Ministries for the Lord

A Resource Guide and Directory of Catholic Church Vocations for Men

Third Edition

PAULIST PRESS
New York • Mahwah

The National Conference of Religious Vocation Directors (NCRVD) in cooperation with Paulist Press prepared this edition.

The National Conference of Religious Vocation Directors (NCRVD) is a collaborative effort of religious women and men working in the vocation ministry for the Church. Its primary concern is the professional training and personal growth and support of vocation directors of religious communities. This concern is, ultimately, a concern for church vocations themselves.

To accomplish this NCRVD coordinates the work of member associations in Eastern, Central, and Western U.S.; cooperates with other national groups on vocation issues; sponsors workshops, programs and a national convention; provides audio-visual and printed resources on current vocation issues; publishes a newsletter and a national quarterly journal, CALL TO GROWTH/MINISTRY.

NCRVD provides a way for the leadership in the Church to further religious vocations. At the same time it is a vehicle for the collective experience of vocation directors of religious communities of men and women to be made available to the Church. NCRVD hears from and speaks to the Church.

For further information contact: NCRVD, 1307 S. Wabash Ave. Chicago, IL 60605.

Coordinating Editor:	Sister Jeanne Schweickert, SSSF
	Executive Director, NCRVD
Associate Editor:	NCRVD Staff
	Mary Ann Hamer
Project Director:	Donald Brophy
	Paulist Press
Book Design:	Celine Allen

Library of Congress
Catalog Card Number: 85-60418

ISBN: 0-8091-2724-5

Published by Paulist Press
997 Macarthur Blvd., Mahwah, N.J. 07430

Printed and bound in the
United States of America

TABLE OF CONTENTS

"Come and See"

"If you don't know where you're going, any road will get you there!" That line from "Alice in Wonderland" always catches me short. How often I've found myself on the road and keep plodding along like I'm headed toward the rainbow. Then somehow I come to a juncture in the road and wonder which path to take. Where am I going? A question not unlike the one Jesus asked the two disciples who followed him, "What are you looking for?" (John 1:38)

Among my possessions is a small paperback, its 64 pages now somewhat tattered and yellow, its cover design faded and marred from its wanderings with me these past ten years. At times when I come to the juncture on the road I thumb through it and THE DESERT IS FERTILE inevitably speaks a message to me. Today it spoke of journey and companions.

> "Whatever conditions you live in, care for you and yours but refuse to be locked within the narrow circle of your immediate family. Decide to take on the whole family of humankind...in loving your country and your own cultural environment, try not to feel a stranger anywhere else in the world...

> "Setting out on the road is not covering miles of land or sea... It is first and foremost opening ourselves to other people, trying to get to know them, going out to meet them... It is possible to travel alone. But the good traveller knows that the journey is human life and life needs company. 'Companion' means, one who eats the same bread. Happy are they who feel they are always on the road and that every person they meet is their chosen companion. The good traveller takes care of the weary companions; guesses when they lose heart; takes them as they are found, listens to them. The companion intelligently, gently, above all lovingly, encourages them to go on and recover their joy in the journey.

> "To travel for the sake of travelling is not the true journey. We must seek a goal, envisage an end to the journey, an arrival....Setting out means to get moving and help many others get moving to make the world juster and more human."

There are many calls and there are many companions for the journey. The book you are now reading, MINISTRIES FOR THE LORD, is about journeys and companions. It offers you the vision of people who have committed themselves to set out on the road, to listen for the voice of the Lord in the world about them, to walk together in joy and pain, to be companions.

This book invites you to reflect on your own journey in life, to ask yourself the challenging question of Jesus, "What are you looking for?" As you spend time reflecting on the various ministries spoken of in these pages, be attentive to the stirrings in your own interior. Those inner movements can be clues to what you are looking for. Make notes and jottings as to what strikes you. Spend time in prayer with these inner urgings, with the person you know you are—your gifts, talents, interests and with the needs you see around you. Ponder all of this carefully. You may recognize the voice of the Lord saying to you, what he said to the disciples, "Come and see." (John 1:39)

The Many Ways of Vocation

The Witness of Religious Life

What Is Religious Life?

From the beginning of Jesus' public life, he called people to come with him, to preach the words of love, healing, forgiveness. This call continues to be answered today through every individual who responds with love to the needs of his or her brothers and sisters.

New Testament stories indicate that some people responded to Jesus' call by leaving home and family, selling everything they owned and joining others who wanted to make prayer and service the focus of their life. Passages like the call of the first four disciples (Mark 1:16–20, Matthew 4:18–22, Luke 5:1–11) and the call of the rich man (Mark 10:21, Matthew 19:21 and Luke 18:22) give us examples of early experiences of a "religious lifestyle."

Historically, certain ways of life emerged from the experiences of men and women who lived in communities concentrating on living the values of loving service, sensitive listening and simple living. Religious men and women make these values their central concern.

All people implicitly try to be their best selves, striving to grow spiritually and emotionally. Each person has within him or herself the ability to be open to events, people and things necessary to discover the range of possible ways of life, accepting the message of Jesus and following Him in their own way. Many people remain within the context of home, family and work and spread the spirit of Jesus through family life and support. Religious men and women "go on the road," leaving home, joining religious communites for support and prayerful living, offering their time and energies in service to a wide variety of people in the setting of their life and work.

Religious make vows as a public statement of their attempt to live simply, concentrate on careful listening to the word of God and loving all His people. The vow of Poverty is a commitment to share all things, both materially and spiritually, to live a life uncluttered by personal possession of material things. The vow of Celibacy is not a denial of sexuality, but in freedom, calls a Religious to be responsive to the needs of the Church wherever and whenever he or she is asked to respond. A Religious enjoys the fullness of relationships, welcoming the chance to grow in self-knowledge and knowledge of others. Obedience is a listening vow, challenging a Religious man or woman to be open to and aware of the changing needs of the world. This might bring a Religious to mission work in foreign lands, parish involvement, teaching, pastoral ministry, health care, and a variety of other ministries. The possibilities are as limitless as the people with whom Religious serve.

How Do Orders or Congregations Differ from One Another?

Most groups of religious were founded at a time in history when travel and communication were very limited. Many congregations were founded at the same time for the same purpose, but in different places by people who didn't know each other.

Founders had a specific spirit or charism they wanted to develop in their community (such as hospitality, simplicity, or unity). This charism, the specific ministries of the community, and a varying emphasis on prayer and community life are the basic differences among religious communities. All are alike in that their primary concern is the spread of the Gospel message of Jesus.

How Does a Person Become a Member of a Religious Community as a Religious Priest or Brother?

The formation program for becoming a religious priest or brother today involves several stages. While these vary from community to community in name, length of time, and format, the following outline is offered as a general view of formation programs.

Contact: A person of high school or college age or older who is interested in religious life but still searching for the answer to the question: "What does God want of me?" could join a program of "contact" with a religious community. This is usually a very flexible program whereby the person meets with a priest or brother on a monthly basis and shares in experiences of prayer and community life with the priests and brothers of the community in which he is interested.

Candidate: A more formal relationship with the community occurs when the young person becomes a candidate. At this time he lives with the priests or brothers while continuing his education or work experience. This period of time enables him to observe and participate in religious life from the "inside." It also gives the community an opportunity to see if the candidate shows promise of living the life of the community. A person may be a candidate for one or two years.

Novice: The Novitiate follows as the next stage of formation. This is a special one to two year period which marks the person's official entrance into the community. A novice spends time in study and prayer, learning more about himself, the community, and his relationship with the Lord. At the end of the Novitiate he prepares for temporary promises.

Vows: Promises of poverty, celibacy and obedience may be taken for one, two, or three years depending upon the decision of the individual person. These promises are renewable up to nine years. Final vows could be made after three years of temporary promises.

A man studying for religious priesthood also has the seminary training of theology, where his time is spent studying the Bible, the teachings of the Church, and the skills he will need to be a priest.

The Priest—Ministering through Sacrament

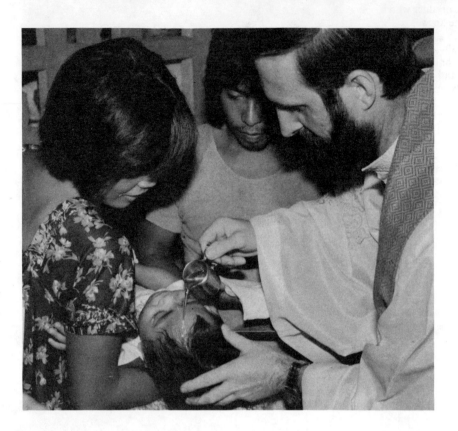

A Priest Is Called By God...

...and sent by the Church to proclaim and teach the Gospel to all people. As one of God's representatives, he administers the sacraments and encourages all Christians to actively participate in the life of the Church. Just as God sent His Son, Jesus Christ, to bring freedom, hope and love to the world, a Priest, in Christ's footsteps, must do the same.

In the beginnings of the Church, Jesus instructed his followers to "go make disciples of all people." In the same way, a Priest is called to enable other Christians to become bearers of the Word, sources of love for those who hunger for justice, love and attention. In order to lead people to a deeper appreciation of human life and of God, a priest acts as a catalyst, urging others to read and learn the Scriptures. He recognizes the need to invite people to become co-workers with him in living and proclaiming the Good News of Jesus.

Being of service to others in a deeply caring way is one of the challenges of the Scriptures. By proclaiming the words of Jesus, a Priest is called to witness to the words of Jesus to be "poor in spirit, hungry for justice, loving, a peacemaker, a servant of the people."

A Diocesan Priest Is...

...a man who responds to his call to Priestly ministry in the context of a particular diocese, and ordinarily serves in that diocese. Diocesan Priests work primarily in parishes, but there are opportunities for other types of ministries, including teaching and mission work.

However, the main difference between a Diocesan and a Religious Priest is that a Diocesan Priest does not profess the vows of Poverty, Celibacy and Obedience that Religious Priests do. A Diocesan Priest does, however, make a public promise to his Bishop to live a celibate and obedient life of service to God and his Church.

A Religious Priest Is...

...a man who becomes a member of a Religious Order or Congregation by having professed the vows of Celibacy, Poverty and Obedience. For him, the Religious community provides strength, encouragement and support for his active ministry. Because Religious communities serve in many dioceses and even in many countries, a Religious Priest does not necessarily remain in a particular diocese all his life as do Diocesan Priests.

Celibacy, In A Spiritual Context, Enables A Priest To...

...consecrate himself totally to God for the service of humanity. Through celibacy, a Priest sets aside the responsibilities of marriage and family life in order to take on the challenge of serving the wider family of God's people.

Through his personal relationship with God in prayer, the friendship and support of fellow Priests, and his many friendships with married and single men and women, the Priest grows in love and becomes better able to serve God's people more effectively.

The Call To Priesthood Is A Challenge...

...to respond with loving service. It requires the ability and willingness to continue to grow and learn about self, others and God. Priesthood offers an individual the opportunity to take an active part in building community, providing an atmosphere of care, healing the loneliness of a fragmented world, making the Eucharist an important part of daily life. The demands are many, but the rewards of service are endless.

For More Information, Contact...

...any Diocesan or Religious Priest, a Diocesan Vocation Director or the Vocation Director from any Religious community. They can answer your questions and help you with the steps toward making your decision.

The Brother—Building Unity

A Brother Is...
...a man who chooses to live out his Christian commitment in community with other vowed men. His life is centered in prayer and dedicated to witnessing to the love that God has for each and every person. In a world of fragmentation and loneliness, Brothers are builders of unity, affirming the reality that all men and women are members of the same family of God. Through the vows of Poverty, Celibacy and Obedience, a Brother chooses to be a living reminder that the message of the Gospel is still and always will be relevant in the modern world.

The three major characteristics of a Brother's life are prayerful community, vows and service. Just as Jesus gathered His disciples about Him and worked closely with them, religious Brothers strive to do the same, giving and receiving the mutual support that comes with fraternal community living and service to God's people.

The vow of Poverty beckons a Brother to live a lifestyle that challenges the emphasis on consumerism found in modern society. A Brother can be a sign that the accumulation of material things does not define the worth of an individual.

Celibacy is commitment to total love of all God's people. It is not a denial of sexuality, but in freedom, allows a Brother to be responsive to the needs of the Church wherever and whenever he is called to respond.

Obedience is a listening vow, reminding a Brother to be open to and aware of the changes in the world and the church. Through his vow of Obedience, a Brother is continually called to discover, through prayerful listening with his community, what God is calling him to and how he can respond.

A Brother Puts His Talents And Skills To Work...
...by responding to people's needs wherever he finds them. Some groups of Brothers devote themselves almost exclusively to one type of work like education or health care. Staffing high schools, lecturing at universities, and working in medical facilities have long been valued ministries for communities of Brothers.

Today, Brothers do every type of work imaginable. We find Brothers in pastoral work, some on missions, and others in professional services like law. Some Brothers become involved in working with the poor, analyzing social and political trends through a political science career, functioning as economists, developing religious programming in cable TV systems, or addressing nutritional concerns through food service planning. Others use their skills in carpentry, mechanics, and agriculture. The areas of service are wide open depending on an individual's talents and the community chosen.

However, it is not the kind of work a man does that describes his life as a Brother, but rather the way he lives. A Brother is a man who needs quiet time to pray, to read and to sift through the significance of his daily life. He is also a man of good humor and joy, someone who welcomes the opportunity to celebrate life's events with his Community and the people he serves.

There Are Different Kinds Of Brothers...
...filling a multitude of needs in today's Church. That is why it is so important to make inquiries about different Communities of men. In some cases, Communities include both Brothers and Priests while other Communities are made up entirely of Brothers.

Every Community Has Requirements...
...related to the Religious lifestyle and ministry. You should be in good physical and emotional health, free from debt, of good character and single. Professional requirements vary. In a teaching community a university degree and a teaching certificate are necessary. In a nursing community, a nursing certificate is required. Some communities offer full or partial educational grants, while others prefer that you complete your professional training before entering.

For More Information, Contact...
...any member of a Religious community or your Diocesan Vocation Office. You don't have to make your decision alone. Members of Religious Communities can answer your questions and give you any additional information you may need.

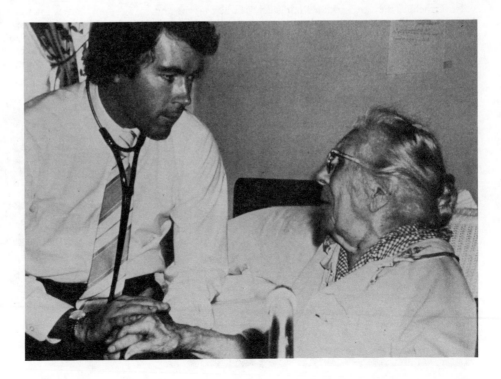

Permanent Deacons

"Ordained Ministers of the Word, Liturgy and Charity"

"For the nurturing and constant growth of the People of God, Christ the Lord instituted in the Church a variety of ministries, which work for the good of the whole body. From the apostolic age the diaconate has had a clearly outstanding position among these ministries, and it has always been held in great honor by the Church."

—*Pope Paul VI, On the Diaconate*

Deacons have been present in the Church from the very beginning. In the first Christian centuries the diaconate was recognized as a distinct and important ministerial order continuing, as Ignatius of Antioch said around 100 A.D., "the ministry of Jesus Christ." Deacons played a major role in proclaiming the Gospel, in liturgy, and in works of charity on behalf of the poor and needy.

Gradually, however, the diaconate declined. By the Middle Ages, for all practical purposes there no longer were *permanent* deacons in the Western Church. Instead, deacons were men preparing to become priests; the diaconate was only a stage on the way to priestly ordination. This remained the state of affairs until the present.

Interest in the possibility of restoring the permanent diaconate began to emerge before the Second Vatican Council. The Council itself approved the idea, while leaving it to national conferences of bishops to decide whether to introduce the permanent diaconate in their countries.

The U. S. Bishops voted to do so in 1968. Since then the permanent diaconate has become a dynamic, fast-growing part of American Catholicism. Sixteen years after its restoration some 144 dioceses had diaconate programs, and there were nearly 7,000 permanent deacons in the United States with close to 2200 candidates in training.

Sometimes permanent deacons are incorrectly called "lay" deacons. It's easy to see why. Except for liturgical functions they do not wear distinctive garb. Most are family men with full-time secular jobs.

Nevertheless, they are ordained ministers, just like priests and bishops. A basic reason for restoring the permanent diaconate is that this fills out the three-fold "hierarchy" of orders—bishop, priests, deacons.

Three general headings sum up diaconal work—the ministry of the Word, the ministry of the liturgy and the ministry of charity.

As minister of the Word, the deacon's most solemn tasks are to read the Gospel and preach. This ministry can also include many other catechetical activities—adult religious education, convert instruction, campus ministry, the religious instruction of children and young people, etc.

As minister of the liturgy, the deacon has a number of official functions in the Eucharistic liturgy. Deacons are also ordinary ministers of the Eucharist and may officiate at Benediction, Baptism, marriages, wakes, funerals, burial services, etc.

As minister of charity, the deacon has a vast potential field for service. Deacons minister in such varied settings as hospitals, old people's homes, schools, prisons and rehabilitation facilities. They work in the inner-city, in rural areas, on Indian reservations, wherever there are people in need.

Permanent deacons come from many different occupations as well as racial and ethnic backgrounds. The diaconate is open to both married and single men, although single deacons may not marry after ordination, nor may those who become widowers remarry. The standard minimum age for ordination is 35, but permission for ordination at 32 and a half can be granted with the approval of the Holy See.

While there are no minimum educational requirements for the diaconate, candidates must obviously be able to handle the program of studies. This normally lasts three to four years—in some cases, three years before ordination and one year after—and includes courses in theology, scripture, canon law, homiletics, communication skills, counseling, etc., as well as field experiences of various kinds. Continuing education after ordination is encouraged and in some places required. Spiritual and pastoral formation are also essential parts of every diaconate program.

A married deacon's wife has a crucial role in the success of his ministry. A supportive attitude on his wife's part is therefore required for a married candidate to be admitted to a training program. Diaconate programs also make it a point to provide opportunities for wives to share as fully as possible in their husbands' experiences of study and spiritual formation. This provides the basis of making an informed consent to her husband's ordination for the service of the Church which is canonically required of the wife of a married candidate of the diaconate.

Lay Ministry

Today many lay Catholics find themselves involved with questions regarding their own participation in the ministry of the Church. While not seeking to enter the vowed life or the priesthood, these men and women seek ways to live their Christian discipleship through church ministry.

How are persons called to lay ministry? What spirituality sustains them? What does their ministry involve?

Call/Vocation

To be called by God is to experience a deep and personal stirring within one's soul. All who believe in the person and power of Jesus, all who are baptized, are called to walk with their brothers and sisters on their journey to the Lord. This is an open call, a call to all Christians. All Christians have a vocation.

As we come to discover our gifts, we are called to share them, to build up the body of Christ which is the Church. The particular call to lay ministry flows from this realization. Since Vatican II, the Church has issued a special challenge to lay persons to reclaim their vocation, to live their call to service and actively participate in the building of the Kingdom.

Spirituality

Call and vocation are ongoing and require an ongoing response. The lay minister enters a life-long conversation with God in prayer. Prayer may be a dialogue with the Lord. Prayer also is a posture of listening, a very still attention to the movement of God in the events of life.

An attitude of Christian stewardship is a central attribute of the spirituality of a lay minister. This attitude causes him/her to care with less control; to create and instigate; to nurture what has been created; to let go, at just the right time, of what has been created.

Sharing in community, be that community the family, the neighborhood, a basic Christian community or the whole community of believers, is an element of the spirituality of the lay minister. Through this sharing, support is generated, a mutual mode of church is recognized, gifts are affirmed, ministries are claimed.

Ministry

Three kinds of lay ministry might be described...

Christian Service or Witness in the World–All baptized and confirmed Christians are responsible in their day-to-day life to witness to the Gospel and serve each other in love. This is the ministry of all the laity.

Volunteer Church Ministry–This type of lay ministry is open to people in most parishes of dioceses. It extends Christian service beyond what is done as a style of living to service or ministries performed in the name of the Christian community in response to the needs of the Church. This type of lay ministry includes men and women who are extraordinary ministers of the Eucharist, lectors, cantors, parish council members, etc.

Professional Lay Ministry–Some lay ministers have as their primary work some type of church ministry. This is their occupation which often requires special training and more formal ministerial commitment to the Church. Such lay ministers might serve as youth ministers, family ministers, liturgical ministers, campus ministers, administrators, planners, etc. These lay ministers are hired to perform particular services that meet a specific need of people and of the mission of the Church.

If you are interested in the possibility of lay ministry, please contact your parish priest for further information or contact your local vocation office.

Black Priests, Brothers and Deacons
"The Time for Harvesting Is Now..."

The Greeks had the idea of time as "opportunity." It was pictured as a man with one lock of hair, but the back of his head was bald. The idea was that as he moved by, you had to catch that one lock of hair, because if you missed it, it was gone forever.

This same sense of taking advantage of present opportunities lest they be missed forever may be one of the reasons there is in the Church a chronic sense of time urgency regarding Black vocations.

There are 1.2 million Black American Catholics, and many of them are affiliated with the nearly 1600 predominantly Black parishes in this country. The numbers of Black priests, deacons and religious brothers is still disappointingly very small. For example, out of a total of 56,000 priests in the U.S. only about 350 are Black. The challenge to the Church today in the Black community is to become truly Incarnational: Black Flesh, Black Spirit, Blackly Christian.

Culture plays a tremendous part in minority evangelization and vocational recruitment. Its values cannot be overestimated. Presently with so few Black priests, brothers, deacons and sisters, the Black community still depends on dedicated and generous White missionaries. It is imperative that those Whites who serve the Black community be up-to-date regarding the sociological and cultural dynamics of the people to whom they minister. Their role is to be enablers and their task is to develop Black leadership in all levels of the Church. Otherwise Black people, particularly youth, will hardly be inclined to dedicate their lives to a ministry in a Church which they perceive as white.

Without authentic cultural adaptation evangelization and recruitment of religious vocations in the Black community is doomed to failure. This authentic cultural adaptation includes, but is not limtied to, Afro-Americanization of the Liturgy wherein music, preaching, praying, vestments, symbols, and design of the worship space, reflect the traditions of the Black American. It includes the development and utilization of religious education programs and resources which are attuned to the sociological, pedagogical, and historical dimensions of Black learners, adult and youth.

And, of course, no discussion of Black religious vocations in the Roman Catholic Church in this country can be considered realistic and serious without acknowledging the institutional and individual racism which permeates this society and Church. Anyone who thinks that the lack of Black vocations can be resolved merely by sending out more invitations to minority persons is a candidate for residency in Alice's Wonderland. Racism is perhaps the single greatest impediment to the increase in Black Vocations.

All the other adverse factors which affect White vocations also affect Black vocations, but racism merely compounds the lack of attraction for the latter. In 1979 the National Conference of Catholic Bishops promulgated a Pastoral Letter on Racism entitled *Brothers and Sisters to Us,* in which they honestly dealt with this issue of racism in the Church. In their pastoral they stated:

> We urge consideration of the evil of racism as it exists in the local Church and reflection upon the means of combatting it. We urge scrupulous attention at every level to insure that minority representation goes beyond mere tokenism and involves authentic sharing in responsibility and decision making (p 12).

This point is so important if Black Catholics are to see this as their Church too. Roman Catholicism has so very far to go in regards to affirmative action. Where are the Black archbishops and ordinaries? (There are presently 10 auxiliary bishops who are Black.) If Whites can serve as heads of dioceses which include Blacks, Hispanics, Asians and Native Americans, why cannot

D.J. Zehnder, Newark Advocate

Blacks and these other minority ethnics do the same? The attitude that Blacks can serve only where there are Blacks is a subtle racist attitude, and Blacks take note of these attitudes.

Vocation literature must also be addressed to and reflect a Black perspective in its invitation. Once the candidates are recruited, racism must be dealt with within the seminary walls and the institutions of theological and pastoral education. In their pastoral letter the bishops addressed this issue:

> Training for the priesthood, the permanent diaconate, and religious life should not entail an abandonment of culture and traditions or a loss of racial identity but should seek ways in which such culture and traditions might contribute to that training. Special attention is required wherever it is necessary to correct racist attitudes or behavior among seminary staff and seminarians. Seminary education ought to include an awareness of the history and contributions of minorities as well as an appreciation of the enrichment of the liturgical expression, especially at the local parish level, which can be found in their respective cultures (p 12).

People must worship and hear the invitation to serve in the ministry in their own cultural language. Their own traditions must be respected and incorporated in all phases of evangelization. When Jesus was looking for men to continue his work he chose his Apostles and numerous other witnesses from among the people of Judea and Galilee, an indigenous group who knew their own; people who were familiar with their goals and aspirations, their dispositions and attitudes. Indigenization was His *modus operandi.* Surely we can't have a better plan than His.

The Hispanic Ministry
"To Convey an Attitude of Love and Kindness"

"Amar es entregarse, olvidandose de si..." To love is to give oneself in selfless service to others. This is the heart of the Christian message. Many have chosen especially to serve the Hispanic peoples of the United States in such a lifelong commitment.

Hispanic people have traditionally been faithful to the Church. Somos un pueble de fe. Families have been successful in handing down Christianity from generation to generation. But tradition and family custom are not enough—for today the faith is being threatened on every side.

Different religious denominations or sects search out and win them over. Young people seek and often do not find a spiritual direction in their lives. Unfortunately some Hispanic intellectuals and college-educated persons abandon the official Church altogether. Recent immigrants from Latin American countries have found it difficult to relate to the North American Catholic Church and society.

Priests and brothers who want to serve Hispanic people are desperately needed. The people themselves ask for their own padrecito who can not only speak their language but who can also understand and appreciate at a deep level what is unique about the Hispanos, what the strengths and weaknesses of their culture are

and what exactly are their cultural values and traditions, their hopes and aspirations.

The Hispanic peoples (the Mexican Americans, Puerto Ricans, Cubans, and others) have a variety of needs. These are signs for the Church as to what it must do in order to relate to its people. Hispanics in the United States are generally poor. Some are migrant farmworkers who cross many state lines in search of work, work which is hard and tedious, which few would choose to do and which often pays below the minimum standards. Others are the urban Hispanos who must cope with crowded living conditions and inadequate school systems. Still others are the recent immigrants who confront a new and strange land with its problem areas such as housing, health, education and rehabilitation in jails and prisons.

In the light of these needs, there is much the priest and/or brother can do to help the Hispanos. A priest as a messenger of Christ, for example, provides the guiding light through clear and forceful preaching and in his way challenges the Hispanic people to be the masters of their own destiny, to develop leaders from their own barrios and to dream dreams they heretofore were afraid to dream. As spiritual leader, he gathers the people around the table of the Lord to celebrate the Christian experience with all its joys, struggles, tears and victories. The brother as servant is available in all situations and is the hand of God reaching out to those in need. Together they pray in the name of the people to the Father for whatever aspirations the community has and represent the presence of God in all critical moments.

If there was ever a moment in which the Hispanic peoples are in need of a Gospel presence, it is now. There are an estimated 20,000,000 Hispanics in the United States. This represents at least 25% of the Catholic Church in this country. At present less then 2% of the priests are native Hispanics. Hispanics are present in all States of the Union and tens of thousands serve in the military both here and abroad.

The Hispanic people of this country need to be affirmed in their cultural identity and to be convinced especially through the Word of God that they are not any less than any one else and that God loves them as much as any other group of people. They must be told that they are a gift of God to the world and they have much to contribute to make this a better world in which to live.

The task of priest or brother is to convey an attitude of acceptance and *carino,* of love and kindness. This is the language that all understand and the communication that builds people up and allows them to see themselves as beautiful and important. All this leads to true liberation of people and permits them to share with others their joy of living.

For those young men who might need it, financial assistance is available through dioceses, religious congregations and through the National Foundation for Mexican American Vocations, founded by Bishop Patricio Flores of El Paso, Texas.

Secular Institutes

What is a Secular Institute?

There is today a growing number of individuals who are becoming more involved in the growth and expansion of the Church and its mission of spreading the "Good News." The laity has responded magnificently to the inspiration of the Holy Spirit who has called certain baptized persons to a life of consecration through the vows of chastity, poverty, and obedience. To give unity and permanence to a particular form of apostolic activity, many souls have sought consecration in an association known as a "Secular Institute," which the new Code of Canon Law defines as follows: "A Secular Institute is an institute of consecrated life in which the faithful, living in the world, strive for the perfection of charity and endeavor to work for the sanctification of the world from within."

History of Secular Institutes:

Consecration as a way of life was practiced from the beginnings of Christianity; men and women, while living in the world and in their own families, took the vow of virginity or celibacy. With the establishment of monasteries and convents, this form of life began to disappear in the fourth and fifth centuries. Vowed persons lived in communities under a particular rule.

Efforts were made to develop associations of consecrated persons who lived at home. Angela Merici in the sixteenth century made efforts to have her followers live a consecrated life in the world. Later during and after the French Revolution similar efforts were made. Consecrated individuals lived in society, while they followed their professions or attended to their work, alongside other men and women, sharing their joys and sorrows, their successes and failures. On May 20, 1938, different groups met in St. Gall, Switzerland, at the request of Pope Pius XI. On February 2, 1947, Pius XII placed the seal of approval on Secular Institutes when he issued the document: PROVIDA MATER ECCLESIA— The Church, far seeing Mother.

Membership in a Secular Institute:

Individual priests, men, women may seek admission in the many Secular Institutes. After a period of spiritual formation, if one is emotionally mature, possesses a balanced personality, and is economically self-supporting, such a person may request to become a member. After professing the counsels, one is considered an official member.

Consecrated seculars wear no religious habit and they are indistinguishable from other lay persons; they go about their daily work in offices, hospitals, schools, factories; they are engaged in different activities. Their one aim is to sanctify their work and their environment by personal witness, transforming presence, encouraging words. They can reach where both priests and religious cannot.

Essential Characteristics of Secular Institutes:

The three essential and distinguishing qualities of this lifestyle are:

CONSECRATION consists of total self-giving by the profession of the evangelical counsels. Obedience offers one's talents to be used for others; poverty offers one's goods to witness the possibility of living among the goods of this world without being attached to them; chastity offers one's love to all without tying oneself to anyone.

SECULARITY focuses on the environment where one lives his/her vocation: living in the world, engaging in activities that belong to the secular order and aiming to direct them all to God's eternal plan.

APOSTOLATE is the ultimate goal of this new form of consecration whereby the members are both a consecration and transforming influence within the world in order to sanctify it and to restore all things in Christ.

Sanctity in a Secular Institute:

Individuals, living a consecrated life as described above, find the strength and courage to live fully their vocation in a deep spiritual life, nurtured by daily prayer, meditation, Holy Mass and Communion; through the sacrament of reconciliation and spiritual direction the consecrated soul is led along the path of a deeper relationship with Christ, whom one will bring to the world in imitation of the Virgin Mary, to whom consecrated souls are especially devoted. A support system is effected through regular contacts with other members, in addition to monthly days of recollection and the yearly retreat.

Each Secular Institute has a very definite and structured formation program that helps in the development of a spiritually mature consecrated secular.

Communication Among Secular Institutes;

Over one hundred and thirty approved Secular Institutes with more than sixty-two thousand members are serviced around the world by the World Conference of Secular Institutes (CMIS) with headquarters in Rome.

In the United States there are eighteen Secular Institutes of diocesan or pontifical right. Liaison is maintained among the members and with the American Bishops through the United States Conference of Secular Institutes (USCSI) which can be contacted at: 3601 Hwy. BB, Madison, WI 53716.

Mimi Forsyth

Religious Communities

S.M.A. Fathers
Society of African Missions

"Building on the Past"

History/Charism

The Society of African Missions was founded in 1856 by Bishop Marion de Bresillac. He was far in advance of his time in missionary thinking and practice, believing that the wholesome values and customs of other cultures must not only be respected, but also integrated into Christian religious practice. He believed that a local Church could best emerge and make use of the elements of a given culture if it was established in the heart of the people. This, he thought, could only be done by establishing a local clergy. In short: "Inculturation."

De Bresillac founded his new missionary Society in Lyon, France on the ruins of an ancient Roman temple. This symbolic gesture has been re-enacted throughout the history of the Society, as it continues to see African priests and bishops build on their own ancient traditions and develop churches that are expressive of the African culture.

Bishop Marion de Bresillac structured his followers into a Society of men, not a religious order, in 1856. Instead of vows of poverty, chastity and obedience, the Society members make a promise to work toward the development of a uniquely African Church.

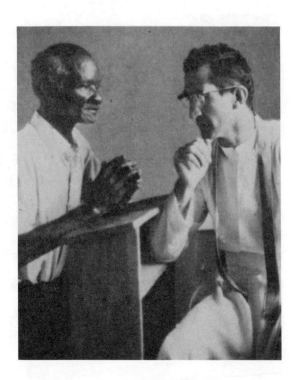

Ministry/Service

The primary ministry of the Society is the training of local clergy. This cannot be directly accomplished until Christianity is firmly established and integrated into the peoples' lives. Therefore, the Society is engaged in the establishment of centers for the training of Catechists, lay leaders, spiritual leaders of small groups, and youth ministers. These can best interpret the Gospel message in a language and terminology that is understandable to their own people.

The Society, working largely in rural, agricultural and fishing villages and in urban areas, is always aware of the material needs of people. It assists local communities with medical, technical, and educational skills and provides personnel to meet their needs.

The primary mission apostolate of the American Province is in Liberia, West Africa and Tanzania, East Africa. It also serves people of African descent in parishes in Newark, Los Angeles, and the Bahamas.

Formation Program

Candidates enter our formation program at Queen of Apostles Seminary in Dedham, Massachusetts. A year's orientation provides a solid foundation in human and spiritual development upon which the S.M.A. candidate can continue to build. From the beginning, candidates work towards an integration of activity and prayer as well as an integration of a sense of mission and the quality of life that is required to be true to their vocation as African Missionaries. African Missionaries must be deeply human and able to relate warmly and naturally to each other and the people they serve.

Each candidate gradually becomes aware in a personal and mature way of what God expects him to be. He learns to recognize and respond to God's action in his life. The formation team guides, affirms and challenges the candidate in this process.

Candidates attend St. John's College in Boston for undergraduate studies, majoring in Philosophy. Postgraduate studies, majoring in Theology, are pursued at Maryknoll, New York.

The Society of Missionaries of Africa

"Internationality-Adaptability-Team Ministry"

History/Charism

The Society of Missionaries of Africa has its origins in North Africa itself. Charles Lavigerie became Archbishop of Algiers in 1867. His passionate commitment to the Gospel and his perception of the changes taking place on the continent at that time led him to found a missionary society dedicated specifically to Africa. From its small beginnings the Society has grown to nearly 3000 members comprised of over 15 nationalities and serving in 25 African countries. Membership can take the form of a life-time commitment (priests/brothers), or a temporary commitment as an Associate Member. Lay Associates engage themselves for a period of 3 years; Priest/Brother Associates engage themselves for 5 years. The type of commitment may vary but all are equally full members of the Society.

Ministry/Service

Our ministry stresses three essential features: *internationality* as a sign of the oneness of all peoples and cultures in Christ; *adaptability* to the language and life-style of the people among whom we work; and *team ministry* in the planning and exercise of our witness and service. Our apostolate includes sacramental ministry, Christian leadership formation, justice and peace, dialogue with Islam, education, basic Christian communities, technical assistance and training, and development.

Formation Program

We consider for membership single, Catholic men between the ages of 21 and 45 who have confronted the meaning of their faith and accepted Christ in their lives. We ask that they have good health and flexibility of character. If accepted into one of the Associate programs they follow a 6 month course of study, prayer and discernment in Chicago followed by an assignment in Africa. Those preparing for ordination or Brotherhood follow a four part program: 1) National Phase: two years of study in the USA. 2) International Phase I: a year of spiritual discernment and initiation into international living in either Zambia or Switzerland. 3) Pastoral Phase: two years of supervised service in Africa. 4) International Phase II: three years of theology and/or professional studies completed by ordination or Brotherhood oath.

Specific Information

Some members of the Society specialize in ministry to the Islamic cultures of North Africa. The majority work in the sub-saharan regions of the continent. The demands of cross-cultural ministry and team work in international communities require an openness to new ways of thinking and doing. We ask our seminary applicants to have finished a minimun of two years of college. Our Lay Associate candidates are requested to have a professional skill as a prerequisite for membership.

Alexian Brothers

A Rich Tradition
A Renewed Vision
Over 650 Years of Healing Ministry

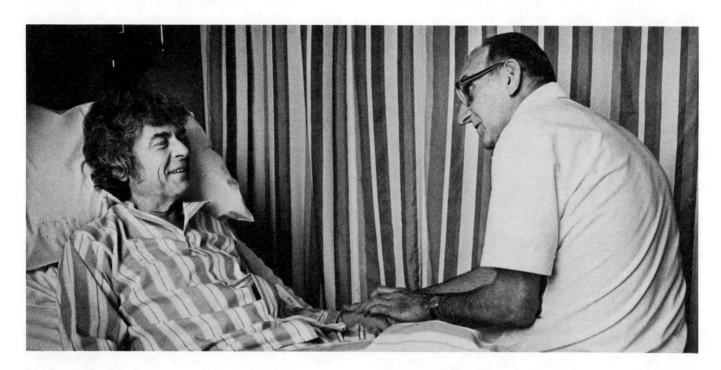

History/Charism

The Alexian Brothers are a religious congregation of Catholic men, whose tradition dates back to the later part of the 13th century. The Brothers, guided by gospel values, continue to provide care for the poor, the unwanted, the sick and the dying.

"The Love of Christ Impels Us" is more than just words. This is the guiding principal of strength for all Alexian Brothers.

Ministry/Service

To Brother is to confront with others the pain and loneliness of existence. There is ultimately no division between the Brother in ministry and those who stand in need of healing.

The Alexian Brothers' charism of caring for people in need has carried forth into the lives and work of today's Brothers. The Brothers minister in general hospitals and life care centers. They also have a mission in the Philippines.

Brothers are involved in all aspects of health care which includes medicine, nursing, administration, clerical, x-ray, and all other areas of health care.

Alexian Brothers are engaged in similiar health care activities in Europe and Africa. Some Brothers serve in ministries not directly sponsored by the congregation.

The Alexian Brothers' commitment of healing is evidenced by on-going and progressive development programs designed to keep each of the Congregation's facilities in the forefront of healing ministry.

Prayer, Eucharist, and community life are an important part of the Brothers' life. Our ministry and Brotherhood evolve from this and we receive daily strength to go forth as Brothers to all people.

The Alexian Brothers' story continues. Their names may change, but the spirit of love, compassion and sacrifice remains. And, of course, there is still much to be done.

Assumptionists
(Augustinians of the Assumption)

"The Coming of Christ's Kingdom for Ourselves and for Our Neighbor"

History/Charism

The crisis of our time reaches back to the last century. The Assumptionists were founded to meet that crisis. Emmanuel d'Alzon, a man of energy and vision, pulled together men to work with him in the work of Christ to rescue God's human family wherever it is threatened. Not a man for the quick fix or stopgap measures, his aim is root causes and the heart of the matter.

Ministry/Service

His brothers and priests are men of contemplative depth, trained insight, competence, initiative and daring. They are to bring the whole bright wisdom of Christ and his gradually unifying Church into the darkness and danger of a world falling apart. Drawing on the rule and spirit of St. Augustine; grounded in prayer, the common life and study; animated by Poverty, Celibacy and Obedience; through teaching, preaching, counseling and consoling; in universities, high schools, parishes, hospitals or on the streets, Assumptionists are to do their part as leaven for the new world that is Peace and God's Kingdom.

Formation Program

Formation is a life-time work for every Assumptionist. For the interested candidate it includes tentative first contacts and a cautious investigation of religious life. Later, as a 'postulant', the candidate spends more time with the various Assumptionist communities to gain the first-hand experience he needs. Novitiate is the first year of religious life itself—a time of prayer, retreat and gradual incorporation into the life of the community. Formal theological and ministerial studies generally follow novitiate, and to these may be added appropriate professional studies and training. Then there are the swift, hard years and the deepening of experience....

Specific Information

Assumptionists are stationed in many parts of the world: around Europe, in Zaire and Madagascar, in Moscow and Jerusalem, in South America, Mexico and Canada. In the United States there are communities in Florida, New York City and Massachusetts.

In a time when the values of an empty culture weaken faith and religious life, Assumptionist initiative calls to men willing to work for new foundations. "If today you hear His voice, harden not your hearts."

Franciscan Friars of the Atonement
The Society of the Atonement

History/Charism

"We joy in God through our Lord Jesus Christ by whom we have now received the Atonement." (Romans 5/11).

Our co-founders, Fr. Paul Wattson and Sr. Lurana White saw the Society of men and women engaged in the work of "at-one-ment", that is, reconciling Christians and their churches, making them one, helping them to reflect their real unity in Jesus Christ who prayed: "...that all may be one" (John 17/21). Begun in the Protestant Episcopal Church in 1898, the Society was received into the Roman church in 1909 and has furthered Christian unity especially through the annual Week of Prayer for Christian Unity begun at Graymoor, Garrison, New York, headquarters of the Society. Today, the Franciscan Friars and Sisters of the Atonement are engaged in diverse ministries for Christian unity and mission throughout the world.

Ministry/Service

The Franciscan Friars of the Atonement operate the Graymoor Ecumenical Institute which conducts workshops, theological conferences and publishes *Ecumenical Trends* and *At-one-ment* newsletter. The Graymoor Christian Unity center welcomes people of all creeds for retreats and days of recollection at our New York headquarters. The Friars have ecumenical centers and libraries in Rome, Italy and London, England. Friars provide the staff for ecumenical agencies in Sao Paulo, Brazil and in Los Angeles and San Francisco, California. They minister at a campus in Los Angeles, CA and serve in parishes throughout the United States and Canada. They labor among Christians and non-Christians in urban and industrial Japan, and poor suburban environs of Kingston, Jamaica, WI. They conduct St Christopher's Inn, Graymoor, for homeless men as well as St. Joseph's Alcohol Rehabilitation Center, Saranac Lake, NY. The experience of At-one-ment is embodied in all our ministries which seek to understand the alienation of humankind and to explore structures for the reconstitution of all peoples at-one with God, nature and themselves.

Formation Program

A young man who discerns the call to reconciliation and unity within himself and for others may also be called to become a Franciscan Friar of the Atonement. There are several stages of Initiation into the Friars which include:

Vocation Discernment: a period of time for seeking the Lord and discovering the most loving response of a person's life. A young man investigates various communities and discerns his best response with a Vocation minister. He attends retreat weekends and has personal contact with the Vocation minister. He applies through a Board of Admissions.

Candidacy Program: a non-residential program for men at least 19 years old and lasting not more than two years. Personal growth and further discernment are emphasized.

Postulancy Program: a residential program at Graymoor, NY of six month's length for men 21 years and older. Growth in communal living is the main goal.

Novitiate Program: a one year experience which initiates the novice into the essential charism and requirements of the community of the Friars. First profession of vows follows.

Post-Novitiate Program: Friars in formation pursue a religious studies program (Brothers) or an academic theology curriculum (Seminarians). Ordinarily, after three years of temporary profession a friar can request perpetual profession or he may extend this period another three years. Opportunities for ministry in missions, ecumenism and our social ministries are provided during the summer months.

Specific Information

All men applying to the Friars must have fulfilled secondary educational requirements. Those seeking priesthood shall ordinarily have completed college, successfully acquiring an undergraduate degree or its equivalent, or be in the process of acquiring such. All Friars will continue to be responsible for their ongoing development and growth for their entire lives.

Augustinian Recollects

"Emphasis on Fraternity and Sharing"

History/Charism

St. Augustine died more than 1500 years ago, but his spirit and ideas were sound—so sound, in fact, that they have attracted followers even to the present time. Augustine is sometimes called "the first modern man" although he lived centuries ago. Even today the story of his journey to God, the *Confessions,* is a bestseller. When he called himself "a restless heart", he spoke for all of us ever pursuing that SOMEONE whom we call God.

This man, known in history as Augustine of Hippo, was the most outstanding convert to Christ and to the Church after St. Paul. His conversion has gripped the imagination of all people who seek God. Some have even sought to follow him and to practice life-long conversion as consecrated religious living according to the *Rule of St. Augustine.*

He lived during a time similar to our own, a period of "breakup" in human history. Overwhelmed by conflicting ideas and religions, the young Augustine's heart cried out for TRUTH and he found it in Christ and his Church. He became a Doctor of the Church and one of the greatest teachers of its doctrines. Among the many gifts which he left to the People of God is the Augustinian "way of Life", a religious heritage continued to this day by the great Augustinian family of which the Augustinian Recollects are members.

Ministry/Service

Our Order, the Augustinian Recollects, is a Catholic community of priests, brothers, and deacons, dedicated to the love of God and neighbor throughout the world. To know us is to love us and the work we do...bringing Christ and His love to the poor, the weak, the aged, the children, the confused, the marginal...in schools and in the "barrios"...in hospitals and homes...in encouraging prayer, study, teaching and preaching among the poor and disadvantaged within the Hispanic apostolate.

Formation Program

Our formation program usually begins in Suffern, New York, where candidates enter the postulancy, a year of acquainting one with the Community. During this year the postulant becomes familiar with our Order and our way of life. He learns about prayer and the nature of religious commitment, and continues his studies.

The postulancy year is followed by a year of novitiate, which is dedicated entirely to spiritual and apostolic formation. It is a year of decision. In the novitiate there are classes in the spiritual life, Scripture, and the history of the Order.

After the novitiate and First Profession of Vows, the friar continues his studies leading to the priesthood or brotherhood. All priesthood candidates must have a bachelor's degree before beginning theology.

Casa Padre Ezekiel Moreno: The Casa is a house of initial formation located in Southern California for Spanish-speaking students who do not speak English or have a high school education. This house of formation exists to cultivate vocations to the religious life. Casa Moreno provides a two-year program to help the Spanish-speaking candidate obtain a knowlege of the English language and to obtain a high school diploma or its equivalent.

Specific Information

The carrier of the Augustinian Recollect charism has been and is the *Rule of St. Augustine.* While the generic characteristic of Augustinianism is interiority, the specific characteristic of Augustinian religious life is dedication to the "common life". The meaning of "the common life" as proposed in the *Rule of St. Augustine* reads: "Before all else you must live together harmoniously, one in heart and one in soul, on the way to God".

Augustinian Recollects are family people and our religious life strongly emphasizes fraternity and sharing. We share a common life of prayer, work, friendship, and recreation. Common life is a way of sharing our personal and apostolic lives in the spirit of the Gospels.

The Augustinians

"Why Do I Speak, Why Do I Sit Here, Why Do I Even Live? The Only Answer Is So That All of Us Might Live Together in Christ"

History/Charism

The discovery of God in his life did not lead Augustine to shut himself in on himself. But rather to pour himself out to others. We who follow him strive to keep this vision alive.

The Augustinians are a worldwide apostolic fraternity established by the Holy See in the thirteenth century. Theirs is the heritage of the religious family founded by St. Augustine in the fourth century.

The foundation of Augustinian life is the common life by which the brothers who are rooted and united in the charity of Christ serve one another, strive to develop the natural talents of the human person by the grace of God, and work for the benefit of the Church and the world.

The purpose of the fraternity consists both in seeking and worshipping God together with one heart in brotherhood and spiritual friendship; and in working to serve the people of God.

The call to Augustinian life is the difficult call to follow the Lord in community of life modeled on the early Christian Church (cf. Acts 2:42-47).

These are the simple and demanding elements of the Augustinian vocation: to live in harmony, intent upon God, with love for the brothers and fellowmen, sharing all things, and to be at the service of the church and our society.

Ministry/Service

The Order is one of apostolic fraternity, that is, a community of brothers who live with the people of God, offering them example in the witness of charity and evangelical simplicity of life (cf. Jn 15:16; Mt. 10; Lk.10). Augustinian ministries include: Parish Ministry, High School Ministry, Spiritual Direction, Prison Chaplaining, Family and Youth Counseling, Foreign Missions, Adult Education and special interest in work among the poor including involvement in Mexican-American housing, an orphanage in Tijuana and a community advocacy program in minority neighborhoods.

Barnabites
Clerics Regular of St. Paul

"Help Us To 'Make a Difference,' Become a Priest"

History/Charism

St. Paul the Apostle is the patron saint of the order and his zeal and piety, centered on the Crucified and Eucharistic Jesus, are the moving forces behind the Barnabites. Inspired by St. Paul, St. Anthony Zaccaria founded the order over 450 years ago in 1530. The Barnabites have been located in North America for thirty years.

Ministry/Service

The Barnabites adapt themselves to the needs of the times and of the dioceses where they serve. A Barnabite is encouraged to be a pioneer, to combine his desire to serve with his own creative drive. Individuality and self-expression are fortified by the community's spirit of fellowship and acceptance as a Barnabite uses his talents throughout the world in many dynamic ways in foreign missions, parish and youth ministries, chaplaincies and spiritual centers. Counted among Barnabites are architects, archaeologists, astronomers, historians, mathematicians, teachers and even a seismologist.

Formation Program

A religious vocation is a special call from God. God does not force anyone to a particular way of life. He invites, He calls using the talents of one's personality. Our obligation is to be willing to respond to God's plan for us. The difference between a vocation and a career is that the latter refers to a job or profession; God's call relates to a way of living out the Christian life. For the man who enters the Barnabite Community the road to the Barnabite priesthood and brotherhood is a unique one, paved with community love and fellowship.

The first stage of formation is called candidacy, a period of discernment to enable a man time to pray and think about God's call to him. This time is spent with an active Barnabite teaching community in Bethlehem, PA. During this time the candidate attends Allentown College of St. Francis de Sales in Center Valley, PA or one of the other local colleges for his undergraduate work. The priesthood candidate decides his own major but must include in his studies some philosophy and theology courses in order to prepare to enter a theological seminary. The brother candidate attends some higher educational institution if he does not already have a trade.

As an alternative to immediate enrollment as a Barnabite, the Self Identity Program is open to any high school senior or graduate. Simply stated, it is a no-pressure, no obligation way to help a young man find out if he is being called to be a priest or brother. It offers a valuable opportunity to discover oneself and one's true vocation through a discernment program of workshops and retreats.

The stage after candidacy is the Novitiate, a one-year period of intense prayer and training which takes place at Our Lady of Fatima Shrine in Youngstown, NY. During this period the novice studies the rules and constitution of the order and strives to understand the commitment which arises from the vows of chastity, poverty and obedience which will be taken at the end of the Novitiate.

Three to five years after the Novitiate the professed student takes the Solemn Perpetual Vows which represent a total and complete

commitment to God for life. This is the end of the formation period for the brother candidate. The priesthood candidate will enter Mary Immaculate Theological Seminary in Northampton, PA after he has completed his undergraduate years and his novitiate.

Basilian Fathers

"Living and Working Together To Spread the Good News"

History/Charism

The Congregation of St. Basil, more commonly known as the Basilian Fathers, is a community of priests and students for the priesthood, one of the many communities called by God and the Church to live and work together spreading the Good News of Jesus Christ and serving the people of God. Basilians live and worship together, striving to be united heart and soul in the spirit of the earliest Christian communities.

The Basilian Fathers were founded in the early 19th century in Annonay, France. They came to North America in 1852, at the invitation of the Archbishop of Toronto, to open a high school in that city.

Ministry/Service

The primary work of the Basilian Community continues to be in the ministry of education, especially the education of young people. In the United States, Basilians have colleges in Rochester, New York and Houston, Texas. They also have high schools in these same cities as well as in Detroit, MI, Oakland, CA, Merrillville, IN and Albuquerque, NM. Parishes in Detroit, Rochester, Houston and its surrounding areas are also staffed by Basilians. There are also Basilians serving in the dioceses of Phoenix, AZ and Las Cruces, NM.

In Canada, Basilians staff seven universities and nine high schools. They are also staffing parishes in Ontario, Lethbridge, Calgary, Saskatoon and Kelowna.

Basilian apostolic involvement also includes work in retreat centers and chaplaincies on university and high school campuses, in hospitals and in nursing homes.

The Basilians continue to work in France where they have a parish and a school and have developed a rather extensive catechetical and evangelization program in Mexico.

Formation Program

Before entering the novitiate, a candidate should, through a period of association, come to know something about Basilian life, and the Basilians should come to know the candidate. The Associate Program is intended to deepen this knowledge and to assist the candidate in determining if he is called to be a Basilian.

Application to become an Associate may be made toward the end of high school or at any later time. Formal incorporation into the Basilian Fathers takes place after the completion of a university degree when the candidate is accepted into the novitiate.

The novitiate year is the formal initiation into Religious Life. It involves an adult decision on the part of the novice to direct his life in a definite way. The primary concern of the novitiate is the spiritual growth of the individual before God and in community with his brothers.

At the end of the novitiate year, the novice professes the vows of chastity, poverty and obedience for a period of three years. The following years are usually given to personal growth in the religious life as well as the formal study of Theology at St. Basil's College and the Toronto School of Theology.

Upon leaving St. Basil's College, the scholastic is eligible for final vows and the call to Orders. After he is called to the Diaconate, the Director of Deacons arranges a program of ministry with each Deacon. The call to priestly ordination takes place after the Diaconate year.

Specific Information

The Basilian Fathers "seek the glory of God in every form of priestly ministry compatible with the common life, especially in the works of education and evangelization" *(Basilian Way of Life, #3)*. Perhaps the call of Christ, "Come, follow Me," will lead you into the Basilian expression of the Gospel of Jesus.

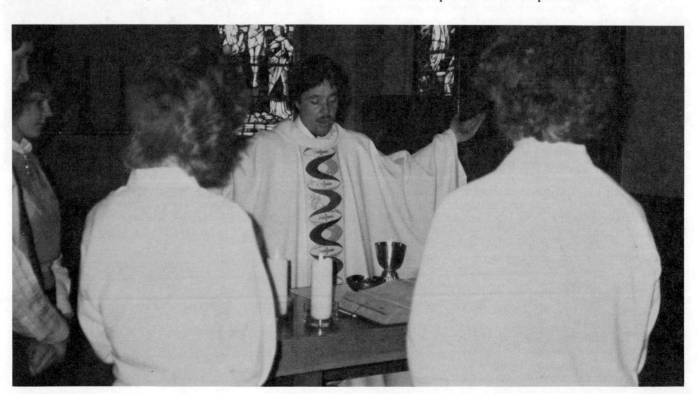

Saint Anselm Abbey Order of Saint Benedict
(Manchester, New Hampshire)

"To Seek God"

History/Charism

Saint Anselm Abbey is a monastic community of the American Cassinese Federation of Benedictines. Founded in 1889, the monastery and college are located on a hilltop overlooking the city of Manchester, New Hampshire.

Saint Anselm Abbey also has a dependent priory in Portola Valley, California, where the monks conduct Woodside Priory School, a college preparatory school for boys.

Seeking God and responding to Him in a life of prayer is the essence of Benedictine living. The monastic life at Saint Anselm Abbey is so ordered as to create an atmosphere conducive to the monk's search for God. The principal means the monk uses in his search are prayer, *lectio divina* (meditative spiritual reading), and work.

The life of prayer is centered on the daily communal celebration of the Eucharist, the Liturgy of the Hours, and *lectio divina*.

It is in this brotherhood of mutual support, respect and charity that we struggle to "prefer nothing whatever to Christ."

Ministry/Service

At Saint Anselm, work is primarily in the field of Catholic higher education. The monks are involved directly or indirectly in our liberal arts college, in teaching, counseling, maintaining the campus buildings and grounds, or as administrators, campus ministers, and staff members. All tasks are holy for the monk who consecrates his entire life for God. It is through this work of service that we minister to the needs of our students, the Church and the world at large.

Formation Program

After gaining some familiarity with the Abbey via correspondence and visits as a guest, a prospective candidate may spend a month's OBSERVERSHIP in the Abbey in order to familiarize himself with the daily rhythm of the monastic life.

The observer phase is followed by the POSTULANCY, during which time the candidate spends several months participating in the monastic rhythm of prayer, *lectio* and work.

During the year of NOVITIATE, the novice is introduced to the foundations of monastic spirituality according to the Rule of Saint Benedict and the monastic tradition. Upon completion of the novitiate and acceptance by the monastic community, the monk begins the three to four year JUNIORATE phase of formation by his temporary profession of the three monastic vows: obedience, stability, and *conversatio morum* (the pursuit of perfect charity according to a monastic manner of life). In addition to receiving personal guidance and conferences by the Junior Master, junior monks pursue formal courses in Theology for a minimum of two years.

It is during this prolonged period of juniorate formation that the monk strives to reach a degree of human and spiritual maturity which will allow him, after prayerful deliberation with the Abbot and community, to respond freely and responsibly to God by pronouncing solemn vows, when the Church receives his total gift of himself, and, in turn, consecrates him to God forever.

Those who feel called and are qualified may, with the approval of the Abbot, undertake studies for the priesthood in order to serve the monastic, collegiate and, at times, diocesan communities by their priestly ministry.

Specific Information

As prospective candidates, Saint Anselm Abbey accepts Roman Catholic men, usually between the ages of 18 and 35. Candidates must be of sound physical and emotional health and must manifest both a sincere desire and the requisite maturity to seek God according to the Rule of Saint Benedict. Entering candidates are encouraged to have successfully completed at least two years of college work.

Belmont Abbey
Order of St. Benedict
(Belmont, North Carolina)

"Seeking God through Prayer and Work in the Benedictine Family"

History/Charism

Belmont Abbey was established as Mary Help Priory by the Benedictine monks from Latrobe, Pa. in 1876. Eight years later, in 1884, it was elevated to the rank of an Abbey. Under the guidance of Abbot-Bishop Leo Haid, O.S.B. for almost forty years, the monks of Belmont established secondary schools in Virginia and Georgia, while laboring in the college and parochial missions of North Carolina.

Today, the monks of Belmont Abbey not only continue the tradition of Benedictine education in North Carolina, but they also strive to be leaders in the Southeast in liturgical awareness in what St. Benedict called "the Work of God."

The Benedictine monks of Belmont Abbey have come together through a personal call from God to imitate Christ in following the rule of St. Benedict. The unique expression of Christian values at Belmont Abbey is made manifest through its Catholic witness in the South, in its consistent daily prayer life and through service to the people of God by education and liturgical life, as well as by Benedictine hospitality.

Ministry/Service

In keeping with the history of Belmont Abbey, the monks have maintained education and pastoral ministry as their principal apostolic commitment.

The monks of Belmont Abbey operate Belmont Abbey College, a four year liberal arts college. Some monks work directly in parishes in North and South Carolina. A number of monks do pastoral service on weekend assistance in the Diocese of Charlotte, North Carolina. Some monks render service to the Diocese through educational, catechetical and liturgical ministries. The monks demonstrate a familial spirit in the care of the Community's sick and aged, as well as guests.

Formation Program

The first phase of the Formation program occurs when a person who is interested in the monastic life, corresponds and visits the Abbey on several different occasions. After time for discernment, the candidate enters the novitiate for a year of specific training in the monastic life. The novice, under the direction of the Novice Master, shares in the daily life of the Community while studying the Rule of St. Benedict as lived by the Belmont monks. After one year, the novice makes vows for three years. Throughout that period, formation continues. The Junior monk continues his studies in the college or begins an assignment in the Abbey. Later, he may begin theological or graduate studies. At the end of three years, the monk may make Solemn profession of vows by which he promises to live a monastic manner of life until death.

Formation is a life-long process. On-going formation is a part of the monk's search for God.

Specific Information

The preferred age range for admission is: 20-50 years of age. The level of education that is preferred by our Community is at least two years of college.

St. Benedict's Abbey
Order of St. Benedict
(Atchison, KS)

"Journeying Back to God to Be Recreated"

History/Charism

Benedictine monks of St. Benedict's Abbey, Atchison, Kansas came officially to the Kansas frontier in 1857. In that year two men arrived from Latrobe, Pennsylvania to establish a Benedictine house which would provide pastoral care for the growing Catholic population. They were to minister out of the supportive environment of a shared monastic life of prayer and work, according to the Rule of St. Benedict. Slowly, over more than 120 years, the Atchison community has made its own the centuries-old Benedictine monastic tradition. We monks of Atchison understand that God calls us to BECOME more than to DO. We are witnesses that union with God is the "pearl of great price". We are called to be searchers after God, to surrender to His love and wisdom. And we must help one another pursue this goal by a generous sharing of our gifts and graces. By daily faithfulness to prayer and work together, we seek to become better listeners to God, more generous cooperators in the "holiness transformation" that Jesus Christ taught must be every Christian's goal. "Be perfect as your Father is perfect." A community strengthened by brotherly love can serve many different needs of the Church.

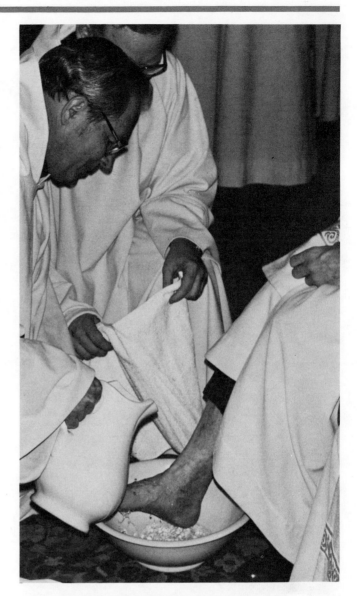

Ministry/Service

Historically, and continuing today, Atchison monks have made education and pastoral ministry their principal apostolic services to the Church. The monks co-sponsor Benedictine College, Atchison, with the Benedictine Sisters of Mt. St. Scholastica Convent. St. Benedict's Abbey also conducts Maur Hill Prep School, Atchison. In pastoral care, several monks serve in parishes of the region either in residence or on weekend assistance. Seven monks do similar pastoral service at a dependent foundation, St. Joseph Priory, Mineiros, Goias, Brazil. Other monks are engaged in ministries or services expressive of their unique gifts. All are engaged in the ministry of prayer and penance.

Formation Program

The formation program of Atchison monks begins with a three month postulancy when the candidate lives in the abbey and shares the daily life of the community under the direction of the postulant director. The postulant leaves the monastery for a period of two months to reflect on his experience and decide if he wants to take the next step as a novice. As a novice the candidate studies the Rule of St. Benedict as lived by the Atchison monks under the direction of a novicemaster. If novice and community discern that the novice seems to have the call of God, he can make vows for three years. Throughout that period deeper formation continues. Indeed, an ongoing formation continues throughout one's lifetime as a monk.

Specific Information

We Atchinson monks vow obedience to our spiritual father, the abbot, as the Rule teaches. We also vow continuing conversion of life—that we will take seriously the commitment to work at yielding ourselves to God through the changing patterns of our life experience. And finally we vow stability. We mean to abide permanently with our Atchison monastic family in its witness to God and service to His Church. We hold ourselves to be willing to share life with our fellow monks in the discipline of searching for God.

Benedictine Monks
St. Benedict's Abbey
Benet Lake, Wisconsin

"Let Them Prefer Nothing to the Work of God" (Rule of Benedict)

History/Charism

The Benedictine way of life began in the sixth century when St. Benedict of Nursia (Italy) wrote his famous *Rule for Monasteries*. The inspiring character as well as the wisdom and practicality of this Rule have been such that it has not only helped guide hundreds of thousands of monks and nuns to holiness, but has been a significant factor in the spiritual and cultural development of western civilization.

St. Benedict's Abbey at Benet Lake was founded in 1945. Abbot Richard Felix, the founding Abbot, was especially dedicated to missionary work as carried out in the Benedictine tradition. For us Benedictines the living of the monastic life in community with its rhythm of prayer, study and work is our principal task. To pray and live the Liturgy is our great treasure. The apostolic activity that flows from this rich spiritual atmosphere helps us to be more genuine witnesses for Christ and to employ more effectively our individual and communal charisms for the needs of God's people.

Ministry/Service

The monks of St. Benedict's Abbey strive to reach out in service to the People of God, especially through retreat work, the apostolate of the press, counseling, helping out in parishes, hospital chaplaincies and a mission monastery in Mexico.

Formation Program

Those men who feel called to seek God in the monastic way of life are invited to spend a few days with us to get acquainted. If a visitor or candidate wishes to join the community and is accepted, he will live as a postulant for six months, sharing in the prayer and work of the monks. He will attend classes in theology, Sacred Scripture and monasticism. When his postulancy nears completion, he can ask to be accepted as a novice. In the novitiate he lives and studies Benedictine monasticism in depth. After a year of novitiate if he believes that God is truly calling him to live as a Benedictine monk, he can request to profess vows for a trial period of three years. These temporary vows can be extended for an additional one, two or three years if it seems advisable.

Following upon this the apprentice monk with the help of God's grace must make a very important decision. If he is convinced that this way of life is his vocation and if the monastic Community gives its approval, he can then make his lifetime commitment to God as a monk of St. Benedict's Abbey with the solemn profession of perpetual vows.

Further studies for the priesthood or for some specialization are arranged on an individual and mutually discerned basis.

Since monastic formation and growth are an on-going, lifetime process, it does not stop at final vows but must be continually worked on and developed by the monk during his entire life.

Conception Abbey
Order of St. Benedict

"A Way to God through Common Work and Prayer"

History/Charism

Since 1873 the Benedictine monks of Conception Abbey have been answering the call to seek God as a dedicated Christian community through common work and prayer. They have been guided in this call by the vision of St. Benedict who outlined a way of following Christ in his RULE, a way which is modelled on Christ's obedience, his humility and service. That monastic tradition was planted in Northwest Missouri by monks from Switzerland and continues to grow and adapt to the movements of the Spirit in their own place and time.

Ministry/Service

The life of a monk is centered upon the Word of God encountered in the Eucharist, the Liturgy of the Hours, the study of Scriptures and private prayer. The day begins with the office of Vigils at 6 a.m. In this quiet and reflective office of psalms and readings, the monk awaits the dawn of the new day in hopeful joy for the coming of the Saviour.

After a period of meditation, the office of Lauds (Morning Prayer) follows. In this office, coming at sunrise, the monk greets the light of Christ, praising God for His goodness. At mid-day, the monks gather as a community for the celebration of the Eucharist. The day's work is brought to a close at 5:30 p.m. with the short office of Daytime Prayer. A period of holy reading precedes the evening meal which is followed by the final office of Vespers (Evening Prayer). At 9:30, the Night Silence begins, lasting until after breakfast the next morning. Night Silence gives the monk the opportunity to pray, study and listen to the Word of God seeking to enter into his heart.

Between the hours of choral and private prayer, the monks work. They are responsible for maintaining their own livelihood as a community and also for serving the needs of the Church within the context of the monastic life. They operate Conception Seminary College, training priests for service in many Midwestern dioceses. They make and sell a wide variety of greeting cards and other types of Christian art through the Printery House. They operate a large farm, orchards and gardens and many work in various crafts and professions that are necessary to support the community of about 90 monks. Some are involved in the very important work of receiving guests and retreatants. Several monks live away from the monastery for study or work in various parish, college and hospital ministries throughout the Midwest. Since 1884 they have also served Sioux Indian missions in North and South Dakota.

Formation Program

The formation program of the monk of Conception Abbey is centered on continuing formation into Christ. The program for candidates and apprentice monks is meant to provide growth and maturity for this in final commitment to the community. Following a period of growing familiarity with the community (the postulancy), the candidate enters the novitiate. During the novitiate year the novice is guided in discernment of his vocation and aided in developing his sense of identity with the community.

After making temporary vows (3-9 years) the apprentice monk continues to grow through a variety of responsibilities, service and studies.

Solemn vows constitute the public and permanent commitment which proclaims the mutual decision on the part of the community and the individual monk that the Lord is calling him to holiness through the monastic life at Conception Abbey.

But formation is a life-long process for the monk. Each day is a new beginning and new challenge for the monk to shape himself and all creation through the power of the Risen Christ active in His Holy Word and in the faith, hope and observance of a monastic community united in brotherly love.

Glastonbury Abbey Benedictine Monks

"Seeking God in All Things"

History/Charism

The Abbey of Our Lady of Glastonbury in Hingham, Massachusetts is a young community of Benedictine monks (founded in 1954) who strive to embrace the challenges of today within the time-tested values of a dynamic monastic spirit. The Glastonbury Benedictine monk discovers and witnesses to the world the loving Presence of God in the ordinary realities of living. The core of the monastic family life at Glastonbury is prayer, both with the community and in private. The daily work of the monks is determined by the needs of the monastery, the church and the larger culture. With faith and perseverance, with a healthy balance of prayer, holy reading, silence and work, the natural rhythm of the monastic life supports and challenges the monk and the community in the search for God.

"By his concern, love and honesty in his dealings with others, he shows that he regards life as a grace, not as an obstacle." (from "A Covenant of Peace: A Statement of Benedictine Life")

Ministry/Service

Flowing from the primary ministry of common prayer for the Church and the world (the daily Liturgy of the Hours and the Holy Eucharist), the Benedictines of Hingham engage in a diversity of services both within the monastery and in the local community. Some of the present works of the community include a ministry of hospitality exercised in the reception of guests and retreatants at the monastery and also in the sponsorship of housing for the elderly and disabled citizens, a ministry of education exercised in various local schools both as classroom instructors and as campus ministers, a ministry of counseling and spiritual direction to other religious and the laity of the area, a ministry of service to the local church by liturgical assistance in neighboring parishes and by preaching, a ministry of mutual service through office and building administration and maintenance, a ministry of availability by responding in community to the needs of the Body of Christ as these needs arise and are perceived.

Formation Program

An inquiry is ordinarily responded to in the form of an invitation to come to visit, perhaps to stay a while and observe. A man seriously considering our community is encouraged to become a candidate. During his candidacy (the length of which is determined by the individual and the director) the individual is open to the experience of community living, receives spiritual direction and guidance.

A period of novitiate follows. This time is a year of intense exposure to the foundations of Benedictine life and the spirit and traditions of this community, both theoretically and experientially. After novitiate, a commitment is made to God in the monastery for a limited time (usually three years). The apprentice monk continues to be guided in prayer, trained in work and study, and is given added responsibility until the decision is made for profession of Solemn Vows, for life.

Further Information

The monastic community life at Glastonbury places a very strong emphasis on personal responsibility and initiative. Each monk, whether a brother or a priest, is encouraged to apply his unique gifts to the service of all, both the community of the Abbey and the community of the church and world. The monk of Glastonbury strives to share the fruits and the struggles of his search for God with other seekers of truth. Guests, retreatants and neighbors join daily in the Liturgy of the Hours and the Eucharist, thus sharing with the monks the gifts of their prayer and service.

Saint Louis Priory
Order of St. Benedict

"Prayer, Work and Community"

History/Charism

Saint Benedict (c. 480–c. 547) wrote a Rule for monasteries, which he conceived as "schools for the Lord's service." Remarkable for its wisdom and moderation, the Rule became standard for monks in the West by the ninth century, and through the centuries down to our own it has guided Benedictine men and women in their search for God.

Saint Louis Priory is a Benedictine monastery founded in 1955 on the outskirts of Saint Louis from Ampleforth Abbey in Yorkshire, England; Ampleforth itself started as the community of Westminster Abbey in London some time before 1066. The Priory was founded at the invitation of the late Joseph Cardinal Ritter, prompted by a group of laymen who wanted a religious community which would operate a school for boys offering a challenging Catholic college preparatory education. The school was opened in 1956. In 1973 the Priory became independent of Ampleforth.

Benedictine monks seek God through a life of prayer, work and community lived under the Rule of Benedict and under an abbot or prior. Prayer is at the center of our lives, and each day includes periods of prayer together and individually. Community means the family life of brothers united in Christ by lifelong bonds of mutual love and service. It is made possible by the Benedictine vow of "stability," whereby a monk commits himself to the service of the Lord in the same monastery for his whole life, and by the fact that we are a relatively small community. (Currently we number eighteen.) Our various works flow out of our prayer and common life in Christ.

Ministry/Service

Our primary ministry is to live our life of prayer, work and community as faithfully as we can. There is sacrifice in this. We believe this is a work for the whole Church. Our chief community works are two: the running of our school, a day-school for about 330 boys in grades seven through twelve with a nationally recognized accelerated curriculum, and the care of the parish of Saint Anselm at Priory, which worships in the Priory church. Both school and parish provide a large number of opportunities for work and service in a wide variety of fields.

Formation Program

There are no age limits and educational prerequisites as such for applicants, although most candidates have completed college by the time they come to us. An applicant usually starts by making several short visits. The next stage is the postulancy, a period several months long for trying out the monastic life. If all goes well, the candidate enters the novitiate, and spends a year under the direction of the Novice Master studying and living the fundamentals of the monastic life. Then come temporary vows, and the beginning of a period of formal study, pursued at an appropriate institution in the Saint Louis area or elsewhere, and structured on the basis of the individual monk's interests and needs, his anticipated work in the community, and whether he chooses to become a candidate for the priesthood. Final vows follow three to nine years after temporary vows.

Specific Information

Each Benedictine monastery is autonomous, although for practical reasons, our houses are grouped in Congregations. Therefore, although all follow the same rule, each house adapts it to its own specific needs. The spirit of each house is peculiar to the house and has to be experienced rather than read about. We have tried to order our life in such a way that we can be fully monks while also bringing full professional competence to our various works—a delicate balance.

Saint Vincent Archabbey Order of Saint Benedict

"The Challenge...The Adventure..."

History/Charism

In 1846, when Fr. Boniface Wimmer, O.S.B., left Saint Michael's Abbey in Bavaria to come to western Pennsylvania, he knew he intended to establish the first Benedictine monastery in the United States. What he did not know was that his monastery would grow to be the motherhouse of the largest congregation of Benedictine Abbeys in all of Western monasticism. Yet from its earliest beginnings, Saint Vincent Archabbey has seen its influence spread through the establishment of Benedictine Abbeys and Priories throughout the world.

The remarkable influence of Saint Vincent Archabbey may well be attributed to the vigorous blend of active and contemplative life which characterizes the community. It is in his HOLY RULE that Saint Benedict defined the dual natures which mark the pendulum swing of his monks' day: ORA ET LABORA: prayer and work. The priest and brother monks of Saint Vincent excitedly set this movement into full swing as they daily dedicate their lives to the glorification of God, as well as to the ministerial service of all men and women.

Ministry/Service

Being a monastery of over 240 monks, Saint Vincent has been able to engage in a variety of apostolic works and ministries. A

college and a seminary on the Archabbey grounds, a preparatory school in Georgia, a campus ministry center at Penn State University, foreign missions in Brazil and Taiwan, as well as 35 parishes in a number of dioceses—all these are staffed and run by the monks of Saint Vincent Archabbey.

Yet the business of the monk's day is balanced by the constant and prayerful seeking of God. Each morning as the rising sun heralds the glory of Our Lord's creation, the monastic community first gathers together, with singleness of purpose, to greet the loving presence of God. Continuing throughout the day, meditative reading of Scripture and private prayer augment the daily celebration of the Eucharist and the communal prayers of the Church's Liturgy of the Hours.

Formation Program

The monks of Saint Vincent Archabbey are keenly aware that the Benedictine vow of CONVERSATIO MORUM (Conversion of Heart) makes monastic formation a life-long process. This ever-evolving process begins for candidates in the novitiate, a year-long period of prayer, discernment, and active living of the monastic life. Classes in spirituality, monastic history, and related disciplines, along with experiential sharing in the "school of the Lord's service" keynote the novices' year.

Following the novitiate, the junior monk professes simple vows to the Order of Saint Benedict at Saint Vincent and begins a period of time, generally three years, during which he progresses in seminary studies and grows in roles of responsibility within the monastery. The junior monk's spiritual development is central during the juniorate as he discerns with increasing certainty his vocation to profess solemn vows to the Benedictine way of life.

These initial years of formation provide the sure foundation upon which the monk builds his life of stability, obedience, and conversion of heart. Each day, each monk wakes to a new beginning which beckons him to further individual growth in authenticity.

Specific Information

As most of the apostolates of Saint Vincent Archabbey are educational in nature, since Vatican II it has been the policy of the Archabbey to accept candidates only after they have obtained a college degree, a trade school diploma, or some other kind of professional training or experience.

Congregation of the Blessed Sacrament

History/Charism
The Blessed Sacrament Community is a worldwide religious order of approximately twelve hundred priests, Brothers, and deacons. For more than a century and a quarter, we have dedicated ourselves to the service of Jesus Christ and humanity through the Eucharist. We were founded in the year 1856 by Saint Peter-Julian Eymard and are today established in one-hundred forty Eucharistic Centers in thirty-four nations.

Obviously, the focus of our life is the Eucharist, especially the Liturgy and prayer before the Blessed Sacrament, wherein we try to interiorize eucharistic values.

Ministry/Service
Our apostolate, too, flows from our understanding of the Eucharist and its demands for Christian living. In the United States, we work largely in pastoral ministry and other fields such as liturgy, retreats and spiritual direction, teaching, writing, hospital chaplaincy, social work, etc. Whatever we do, we try to bring a eucharistic spirit of generosity and Christ-like giving to our work!

We live in community as brothers united by the same ideals and spirit. This increases our effectiveness and offers a sign to the Church and the world of the unity which the Sacrament of Christ's Love is meant to foster. St. Augustine once called the Eucharist "the sacrament of unity and the bond of peace."

Our congregation includes both lay and ordained members; all share equally in the life and mission which we have embraced as religious of the Eucharist. Each individual is educated in a field of special interest or competence, where he achieves his own full human potential and serves the goals of the community and the Church.

We are historically part of a larger *Eymardian* family, one in spirit and dedication with the contemplative Servants of the Blessed Sacrament (for women) and a Secular Institute called "Servitium Christi" (for both women and men).

We have nine local communities in the United States and overseas missions in the Philippine Isles and several African countries.

As Jesus' life and ministry continuously celebrated the love of the Father who sent him, our mission is to live the Eucharistic mystery and all its implications. We PROCLAIM the saving death and resurrection of the Lord and commit ourselves to work for the Kingdom of God, in which all people will experience true LIBERATION and COMMUNION.

Formation Program
Our educational program has three major stages:

1. *Pre-Novitiate:* First, "Candidacy," a non-residential program of contact with one or several of our communities. Lasts six months as a minimum. Second, "Postulancy," actually living in one of our communities to experience our life, spirituality, and mission. "Postulancy" runs anywhere from six months to two years.

2. *Novitiate:* A "time apart" from the normal routine of one's life, the "Novitiate" introduces the individual to our eucharistic vocation and mission. The experience includes prayer, study and spiritual direction, community life, and work in one of our apostolates.

3. *Post-Novitiate:* The "Scholasticate" provides professional/theological training for work as a Blessed Sacrament Priest or Brother.

Camaldolese Monks
Immaculate Heart Hermitage

"Separated from All and United to All"

History/Charism

The Camaldolese monks, a branch of the Benedictine tradition, originated with St. Romuald in 11th Century Italy, and embrace both the communal and solitary forms of monastic life.

In the words of St. Benedict, the monastic vocation is a call "to seek God". Whether followed alone or with other men in community, it is an invitation into the "desert"—the solitude of a man's inner self—for a personal encounter with God. Here the monk is to discover both his own deepest identity and his gift for his fellow man. Here he experiences and becomes a witness to the truth that God alone sustains.

One of the early Desert Fathers said, "the monk is separated from all and united to all". As his heart, his deep "contemplative self" awakens, the monk becomes aware of the boundless compassion of the Father and discovers, even in the ordinary tasks of life, the deep communion that joins all people: it is no longer only he, but Christ who lives and prays and works and suffers in him.

Ultimately, the life of the monk is a mystery not to be explained

but to be lived, experienced. A man recognizes in his inner depths this wordless call and responds—and this response involves his whole person and becomes his whole life.

The Camaldolese life is one expression of this monastic charism. It was brought to the United States in 1958, with the opening of Immaculate Heart Hermitage, also called New Camaldoli, in the Santa Lucia Mountains of Big Sur, California, overlooking the Pacific Ocean.

Ministry/Service

Prayer is the heart of the Camaldolese life, supported by a disciplined life of work, asceticism, reading and study. All of this is situated in the Church of Vatican II: embraced within this life of prayer are the contemporary concerns of ecumenism, social justice and peace.

In the Camaldolese hermitage, elements of both cenobitical and eremitical life are combined. The daily communal Eucharist and Prayer of the Hours provides a basis and framework for the lectio divina, meditation, prayer and study done by the individual monk in his cell. The daily rhythm is varied by occasional meals in common and recreational hikes.

Forms of work are determined by the needs of the community and the aptitudes of individual monks. In addition to the tasks involved in any community life, some of the monks are occupied with the care and guidance of retreatants and visitors, while others work in the bakery or at other productive jobs to contribute to the support of the community.

Formation Program

Monastic life itself constitutes the basic formation program. It is a lifelong journey on which one learns to see and to listen with the heart. To seek God is a search for wisdom, a paradoxical learning which supposes the willingness to unlearn, to let go, to trust—in a word, to open oneself to the transforming action of the Spirit.

During the year of postulancy, the year of novitiate, and for some time after temporary profession (which is first made for a three year period, and then may be extended), the formation is marked by emphasis on communal life. As he lives, works and prays with his brothers, the young monk learns much—and eventually that humble service of love which is the necessary foundation for the life of prayer to which he aspires.

Class instruction during postulancy and novitiate centers on monastic spirituality, with special attention given to Scripture and the Fathers. During the following years the young monk will continue his studies in these and other subjects related to his life. Sometimes a more extensive study of theology or some specialization will require living outside the community for a time. Studies oriented toward the priesthood may be recommended if this vocation is indicated both by the person's own inner inclination and by the judgment of the community.

Specific Information

The Camaldolese hermitage offers a path to the realization of the monastic charism through a unique and flexible combination of communal and solitary life. Persons interested in our way of life are usually invited to come for a week's retreat. Before entering the postulancy, an observership of at least one month within the community is required. For details regarding daily life, admission requirements and retreat facilities, please write.

Carmelites

"Occupied With God in Both Prayer and Work"

History/Charism

The Carmelites became a religious order around 1209 when a group of men living on Mt. Carmel requested a rule from Albert, the Patriarch of Jerusalem. This rule was basically eremetical and ideally suited to life in the Holy Land. When Moslems began to expand their influence and empire, they sought to capture the Holy Places. This turmoil forced the Carmelites to migrate to Europe. In 1238, they came to Messina, Marseilles, Aylesford and Hulne.

The rule so ideal in the east was completely out of sorts in the west. Gradually, the Carmelites modified their way of life from hermits to friars. The rule was mitigated and adapted to western monastic living. Preaching and pastoral ministry became new apostolates. Carmelites began to attend and teach at the universities.

This is what happened to the Carmelites but throughout these difficulties, they maintained the original goal and charism of the order. They were called to "live in imitation of Jesus Christ" and "meditate day and night on the law of the Lord." This cultivation of the spiritual life and active ministry in the church flowed from two sources: the inspiration of Elijah the Prophet, whose twofold spirit of prayer and activity was demonstrated in his activites on Mt. Carmel and Mary, Mother of Carmel, who was always open and aware of God's presence in her life.

To be occupied with God both in prayer and work is the call, the charism of the order.

Ministry/Service

There is no Church ministry that is excluded from Carmelites.

They are actually engaged in parishes, hospital chaplaincies and education. Another classification is individual apostolates. The Carmelites encourage their individual members to utilize their talents in areas where they are qualified for the good of the Church. You will find Carmelites engaged in alcohol education, counseling, drug prevention, bio-genetic research and social work in poverty areas.

Carmelites can serve in any of the mission territories of the order. These include Zimbabwe, Indonesia, the Caribbean, South America and the Philippines.

Formation Program

The Order of Carmelites accepts students after the completion of High School. They attend our Carmelite College Program. They participate in a dual program: education and activities at the college and an experience of Carmelite living at the residence. After college is completed the student enters the Novitiate, the beginning of the Carmelite Religious life. The Novitiate is a year of training in spirituality, self-awareness and the traditions of the Carmelite Order. At the end of the Novitiate year the Carmelite Novice professes vows of chastity, poverty, and obedience. To continue experiencing the life in Carmel the newly professed Carmelite lives and works in one of the communities. Then the student goes to Washington, D.C. for theological studies. At the completion of the theological program the Carmelite Professed is eligible for Ordination. Since our program is flexible the Carmelites try to assess the needs of the candidate. There is no age limit to a person considering the Carmelites.

The Discalced Carmelite Friars of the Western United States

"A Community of Men of Prayer, Serving the Church"

History/Charism

The Discalced Carmelite Friars are a religious order of priests and brothers. They began around the year 1200 as a group of European hermits living together on Mount Carmel in Palestine. They had been drawn to Mount Carmel by its traditional association with a powerful Old Testament figure, the prophet Elijah. They were also devoted in a special way to Mary, the Mother of Jesus, for they dedicated their Oratory to her. Sometime between 1206 and 1214 they received a rule of life from Albert, Latin Patriarch of Jerusalem. By the year 1238, however, political and economic conditions forced them to begin returning to Europe. In Europe their manner of living changed. They kept their contemplative spirit but ceased to live as hermits. They began instead to live a closer community life in or near towns and cities and to minister to the people there. In a word, from being hermits they became friars, much like the better known Franciscans and Dominicans.

During the second half of the sixteenth century in Spain, St. Teresa of Avila began a reform of the Carmelite Order. She started with the nuns (1562), but her reforming work soon spread to the friars (1568). By the end of the century the Discalced Carmelites were established as a completely independent branch of the Carmelite family. *Discalced* means "without shoes", which was a sign of reform in sixteenth century Spain.

The first foundation of Discalced Carmelite Friars in Arizona was made in 1912 by Spaniards who came from Catalonia by way of Mexico; the first in California was made in 1924 from Ireland. Today there are about fifty Discalced Carmelite Friars in California and Arizona living in five different religious communities. Although all of their houses at present are in California and Arizona, the territory of the California-Arizona Province of St. Joseph includes the entire western United States.

The life and ideal of the Discalced Carmelite Friars is one of prayer, community life and apostolic service—all according to the founding inspiration of the original hermits of Mount Carmel and the reforming inspiration of St. Teresa of Avila and her collaborators, especially St. John of the Cross. For the Discalced Carmelites prayer means especially silent, interior prayer; normally one hour is set aside in the morning and another in the evening to express and foster this inner prayer. The Discalced Carmelites also celebrate the liturgy—the Eucharist and the Liturgy of the Hours, or divine Office—in common.

Ministry/Service

Discalced Carmelites live in community and strive to build up relationships with one another that are based on mutual trust, respect and love. They hope to be a sign and source of unity and peace in the world. Finally, Discalced Carmelite Friars are committed to the service of the Church and the entire human family. They labor especially to foster the sense of God's presence and the inner life of the spirit.

They may engage in a variety of works, from giving retreats and spiritual guidance to making known the spiritual teaching of St. Teresa and St. John of the Cross, to counseling, writing and staffing a parish or assisting in one.

Formation Program

Whether entering as a candidate for the priesthood or brotherhood the following initial steps in training are the same for both states:

1. Postulancy, June 24-September 7

2. Novitiate, one complete year, September 7-September 8 (of the following calendar year)

3. Upon completion of the novitiate year, vows of poverty, chastity and obedience are taken for one year, to be renewed each year for five years. The five years of temporary vows completed, these vows are then made for life.

4. Scholastic Formation Year—follows the novitiate year. It is a period during which Carmelite studies are emphasized.

5. Senior College years—approximately two years are allocated for the completion of college. This is required for those studying for the priesthood. Brothers may also pursue this course, or engage in other pursuits deemed appropriate for their vocation.

After completion of college, candidates for the priesthood join the community at Berkeley, California, for four years of theological schooling, leading to ordination.

Brothers of Charity

"Helping the Deprived and Bringing Hope of Salvation"

History/Charism

Rev. Peter Joseph Triest founded the Brothers of Charity in 1807 in Belgium. He possessed a great charism, a driving spirit, to care for the poor and destitute. This charism continues as the inspiration of our response to the needs of the church today.

Peter Triest established his four congregations to meet specific needs—to help the deprived and bring them the hope of salvation. The work of the Brothers and the Sisters of Charity in caring for the blind, deaf, mentally ill, the physically handicapped, and the aged is a sign of God's goodness; through this ministry the poor, the destitute, and the neglected are filled with the hope and joy of the Gospel. Every step in progress is seen as a tangible sign of God's design in their regard. We, too, as brothers, see God's work within us as well in our lives. Thus we are able to share in our founder's charism.

This charism has imposed on us the obligation of upgrading the quality of our pastoral and apostolic effort; bringing the good news to deprived and spiritually impoverished youth; responding to ecclesial responsibility by our concern for the happiness of others; sustaining and supporting our professional impact with charity; motivating ourselves and our colleagues by the spirit of faith in our apostolates toward the sick, handicapped and the elderly. However divergent our tasks as brothers, charity unites our efforts into single unity. CHARITY brings us closer together, inspires initia-

tives, is ingenious and dynamic. It finds ways of bringing God's love to those most in need of it, and of tailoring our lives into a pattern of personal holiness.

Ministry/Service

In the United States, our charism is manifested through the brothers' focus on education, social services, and parish ministry. The brothers currently serve on the faculties of several schools, staff shelters for the homeless, and serve in social service centers in the urban areas of the country. In addition, the brothers are involved in such areas as choir, liturgy, religious education, and CYO committees. In their local neighborhoods, the brothers serve as coaches for athletic teams and are leaders in civic organizations, and Boy Scouts.

Formation Program

Interested men have the opportunity to attend weekend vocation discernment experiences arranged with the vocation director. After such a weekend, the candidate may return for other weekends to observe the day to day life style of the brothers. There are limited instances when a candidate may live with the brothers for a period of time but these are decided on an individual basis. Once the candidate has completed the application process and has been accepted, the postulancy begins which lasts for one year. This period allows the postulant the time to make the transition into a new way of life and tests his ability to live that life. When this period ends, novitiate begins. This two year program is centered on our rule and way of life. It is time given to deepening faith, prayer and personal development. Conferences are given on selected formation topics. Time is afforded each novice to spend in other communities of the congregation as well. Apostolic work experience is an integral part of the program along with theological studies. This program is aimed at helping the candidate decide if he is willing to profess vows in the community at the end of novitiate.

Specific Information

Brothers of Charity, in 16 countries, are men who have chosen to live together in a community of love, sharing themselves in a relationship of obedience, poverty, and celibacy with each other and with the people of God. The brothers are spirit-guided, dedicated men, willing to acknowledge their commitment and to publicly crusade for it. In a life of service, the world can see these men as Christians in action, part of a larger Christian group, bringing to it the benefits of a unique and unusual life style. The highest ideal presented by Christ is not, however, obedience, poverty, and celibacy...but CHARITY. Charity produces honesty and simplicity in a community life of service.

Missionaries of Charity

"Called To Serve Christ in the Poorest of the Poor"

History/Charism

Some years after Mother Teresa had so wonderfully established the work of her Sisters among the poorest of the poor in Calcutta, she was inspired by the need for a group of men who could work in the same spirit. So, on March 25, 1963, a start was made with the Brothers' Congregation. From the small beginning in India the Brothers now have 37 communities in 18 countries in the United States, Central & South America, Asia, Africa and Europe.

In order to give more than mere bread to the hungry, the Brothers lead a life of prayer and have the Mass as the center of their lives, so that they may be a little like Christ who gave His own body and blood so fully and lovingly to His Father and to His brothers and sisters who are so poor in every way. As part of their charism of poverty in living like the poor among whom they work, the M.C. Brothers do not have private rooms, and have limited clothing and personal belongings which are kept on a small shelf. There is no television, radio or stereo. Even the plainly furnished chapel reflects the simplicity of life. They try to live in this poor and simple manner so that they may be free from all encumbrance in their wish to be of service to God and the poor.

The Constitutions of the Congregation say: "Each Brother is called by Christ to serve Him in the poorest of the poor on the streets and slums, in the leprosy patients, the abandoned and exploited, in a word, in those who live in the greatest misery and need. A special mark of our spiritual lives must be the habitual attitude of trying to find Christ in the poor person. For this is one of the clear revelations of the Gospel: *The poor person is Christ.* The poor person is a sacrament of Christ in the world. There is a real presence of Christ in the suffering and abandoned—and we serve and honor Christ when we serve our needy brother and sister."

Ministry/Service

The work of the Brothers in India includes clinics for lepers, the care of homeless boys in the streets, small schools in the slums, and care of the dying and handicapped destitutes.

The work is done in a simple way. The idea of the Brothers is to have a preference to go out on the streets and to the slums to meet the poor and suffering, rather than to run institutions. But some homes and shelters are necessary for the people they meet which they try to conduct in a simple and personal way.

In the United States, the Missionaries of Charity are working with the same spirit among the poor in the affluent part of the world. Here the work is in meeting the alcoholic, the physically and mentally ill on the streets; visiting the old and lonely people in nursing homes and hotel rooms; men in prison, families from Latin America, who have come as immigrants; and in offering hospitality to homeless men, entire families and also runaway boys.

Formation

"Come and See": When a person wishes to try his vocation with us, he may come and live with us for several months. This period, known as the "come & see" is a time in which a person lives with us, shares in our prayer, work, community life, household duties, etc.

"Novitiate": The Novitiate is a two year preparation for Religious Profession of Vows. During the first year, half the day is spent in instructions on the Life of the Brothers, prayer, Scripture, and the spiritual life; the other half is spent in working among the needy. During the second year, the Novice is assigned to any one of the regular communities.

"Profession": After Novitiate temporary vows are made annu-

ally for a period of five years. Then Final Vows are made.

Specific Information

At present we have no age limit for entrance and there are no special educational requirements. The main requirement is that a man have the desire and ability to live a community life of prayer and simple lifestyle, and to dedicate himself to work among the poorest of the poor.

Servants of Charity
The Guanellians

*"Working with the Retarded,
the Orphaned, and the Aged"*

History/Charism

The congregation of the Servants of Charity, often called the Guanellians, was founded in Italy in the early 1900's by Fr. Louis Guanella, Blessed by Pope Paul VI, on October 24th, 1964.

As a young diocesan priest, Father Guanella had a clear vision of charitable and social work for the needy, the retarded, the orphaned, and the aged. Under the impulse of the love of Christ, he spent his whole life and energies for them. However, he was not content devoting just his own time; he sought followers to share and continue his work. These are his religious followers, the "Servants of Charity" and the sisters "Daughters of St. Mary of Providence," who are working in Europe, Israel, North and South America.

Bl. Aloysius Guanella

Novitiate: It is a one year special program which emphasizes the personal, Christian and religious formation of the candidate, with particular regard to his future service among the handicapped.

After Novitiate: The candidate for the priesthood will have four years of theology, then ordination and the first appointment. The candidate for the brotherhood will have a transitional appointment, with the possibility of furthering appropriate educational training.

Specific Information

Candidates are eligible to join the Congregation after they have completed high school.

Ministry/Service

The Servants of Charity are involved in every form of charitable apostolate, in particular:

Caring for the retarded and the aged; educating boys and youth materially or morally needy; practicing the priestly ministry in Parish work.

Formation Program

Pre-Novitiate: A candidate for the priesthood shall continue or complete his college education at the Don Guanella Seminary, Sproul Road, in Springfield, Pennsylvania, 19064. One of these years will be considered as part of the Pre-Novitiate program, which will provide him an opportunity to share in the works and prayer life of the community.

De La Salle Christian Brothers

Catholic Educators for Justice and Peace

History/Charism

The Christian Brothers are followers of Jesus and live lives based on the vision of the Gospels and the New Testament. Jesus came preaching the reign of God whom he called "Father." So, too, we strive to teach others about the reign of God revealed through Jesus. We consider ourselves to be ambassadors and ministers of Jesus Christ in the work we do. We try through words and deeds, in our prayer, ministry, and communities to mirror the love and faith that is the Christian heritage.

We live in community. From our origins, we Brothers have placed a high value on the togetherness of the journey of Christian ministry. Community for us is a place of mutual support in prayer, meals, conversation and celebration. Our communities are also homes where hospitality and fellowship are extended to the larger Christian community which they serve.

The Christian Brothers follow Jesus in the tradition of St. John Baptist de La Salle (1651-1719), a French priest who saw young people hungering for a chance to grow, especially spiritually. He fed that hunger with Christian schools. His life-long work was fired with a love for the Scriptures, compassion for children, and excitement about the Gospel which energized him to put its message into effect in his own day. Attracted by St. La Salle's style, competence and faith, men soon joined him and began living in groups. By living as brothers, they supported, challenged, and prayed for each other. Community seemed to be God's way of helping them reach out unselfishly to serve others, especially the poor. To say publicly how much they wanted to live this way, they vowed to live in community and to teach the poor free of charge. The traditional Gospel vows of poverty, chastity, and obedience were soon joined to these two vows to signify a special and unique religious commitment. In time, the men who banded together in the charism of St. La Salle were offically known as the Brothers of the Christian Schools. The Church has since declared St. La Salle the "Patron of Teachers" and the Brothers "the Apostles of Catechism." We today strive to take up the challenge, with joy and thanksgiving, of Christian Brotherhood for the education of God's children.

Ministry/Service

We are Brothers and educators. We teach about the dignity of labor and the responsibility of wealth; about marriage and relationships; about love, faith, and hope, and especially in our times, about justice. Whether we work with poor or rich, we strive to give testimony to God's justice which is mercy. Our ministry takes various forms. Many of us are educators in schools. Others present the message of Christ and the kingdom through campus ministry, retreats, counseling, missionary service, parish programs, social work and other forms of helping people grow in the faith.

Formation Program

We welcome Catholic men of various ages and backgrounds. An applicant should have an interest in a life of service and should have the skills to accomplish academic and professional courses of study necessary for an educator. Each province interprets the Brothers' ministry in ways meaningful to its own locale and history. There is no one pattern of introduction into our life and ministry. In general, the formation programs offer the following:

social and written contact with the local vocation directors, formal association with the Brothers through formation programs which provide regularly-scheduled personal meetings with a Brother, experiences of service, and residential programs to experience our lifestyle. At some point in the course of his training, a man spends one year in a special program for religious and personal development (the novitiate year). Specific questions concerning the formation process are best answered in consultation with the local vocation director.

After the novitiate we publicly vow chastity, poverty, obedience, and service to the poor through education. By our vow, we declare our intention to live lovingly as Christ did and to do this through our religious community. Our vows help us to live simply and with a spirit of sharing, to respond freely to the Spirit in cooperation with our Brothers, and to teach with a special love and attention to those who are most in need of Christ's healing presence. At first, vows are temporary—professed a year at a time. A life-time commitment comes after several years of experience in the ministry. When we make life-time vows, we profess to remain faithful as a Brother for the rest of our lives.

Special Information

We, Christian Brothers, number close to 10,000 serving in 80 countries. We are exclusively Brothers, laymen who lead lives of prayer and service in a religious community, the largest such group in the Catholic Church. There are 1500 Brothers in nine English-speaking provinces of North America. All Christian Brothers who live in St. La Salle's tradition are part of the same international institute and follow the same religious Rule; each province, however, has its own variation of style and emphasis. Our common tradition has produced a sense of fraternal friendship and a practice of communication and exchange among the Brothers throughout the world.

Our founder, St. John Baptist De La Salle, cared for individuals; he loved persons. We do, too. He lived with enthusiasm; we try to do the same. He was always prayerfully conscious of the presence of God in his life; we hope that we are following his example. He cherished the strength and blessing that communal living brings; we build community among ourselves and among others. We Christian Brothers place ourselves under the New Testament as men of faith, living in community, working in education.

Congregation of Christian Brothers

"Confronting Social Issues Through Education"

History/Charism

Early nineteenth century Ireland suffered from the effects of centuries of religious persecution. The children of the Catholic poor were denied all hope by being denied the chance of an education. Edmund Rice, a wealthy widower, had wanted to dedicate himself to God in some European monastery, but realizing the urgent need of his country's poor, he decided to dedicate his wealth, his energy, and his life to the Christian education of the poor of his time. When other inspired men joined him in his work, and in his religious dedication through the vows of poverty, chastity and obedience, the Christian Brothers began. The example of Christ-like generosity which characterized the Founder of the Christian Brothers challenges the Brothers in the modern world to strive to capture the same sense of urgency and apostolic inspiration which moved Edmund Rice to confront with open mind and heart the great issues of his time.

Ministry/Service

The Brother in the modern world confronts the agonizing reality of the issues of poverty, race, peace, ignorance, social injustice and religious indifference. Faithful to the example of Edmund Rice and with the confidence of Jesus, the Brother is similarly convinced

that his contribution toward improving these existing conditions is in the area of an EDUCATIONAL APOSTOLATE. He feels that he can make a difference because he is aware of a strength that is his when he is joined with other men possessed of a similar sense of urgency in a close-knit praying community. The Brothers operate elementary, secondary, and university schools throughout the world.

Formation Program

A young man prepares to become a Brother by being helped toward the realization of what it means to be a follower of Christ as a Christian Brother. In the American Provinces, this begins with a Postulancy Program during which the aspirant attends college and learns how to form a community with other like-minded men. Next the aspirant does a year's novitiate. This year is an intensive study of the Christian life as lived in a Christian Brothers' community. He then finishes his college education and works for teacher certification. For the man who has already begun or completed college, the formation program is tailored to his specific needs and those of the community's educational apostolate.

Specific Information

The men we seek to join us in this work are Catholics who would like to work closely with young people in an educational apostolate. They are high school and college graduates with the physical and mental capacity necessary for the work and with the psychological capacity to live the close community life characteristic of the Christian Brothers. They are men with the religious inspiration and dedication necessary to live a life of consecrated celibacy, and ready to place all their talents and possessions, through the vows of poverty and obedience, at the disposal of the Community for the sake of the love of God and the needs of their fellow men and women.

Brothers of Christian Instruction

"My Schools Are Established To Spread the Gospel of Jesus Christ."

History/Charism

In 1819, Fathers Gabriel Deshayes and John de La Mennais joined forces to establish the community of the Brothers of Christian Instruction in order to restore dignity to the ministry of educating the poor. The chief aim of the founders was to make known Jesus and his Gospel path to salvation and thereby rescue the young from aimless lives resulting from ignorance and immorality. The early Brothers, teachers of solid piety, proved very successful in assisting the parish priests and in adopting a pedagogy suited to the poor rural areas in the post-Revolution Catholic Brittany section of northwest France. In a short time, the Brothers spread throughout their native region and into the French colonies, e.g., the West Indies, as well as into French-speaking Canada. At the turn of the century, religious persecutions drove them to England, Spain and the USA. At present, all provinces of the institute have established their own foreign missions where Brothers of Christian Instruction can now be found: Japan, Uganda, Tanzania, Kenya, Senegal, Rwanda, Zaire, Burundi, Ivory Coast, the Seychelles Islands, Tahiti, Argentina, Uruguay and Chile. With general headquarters in Rome, the 1550-member community has Brothers ministering in 23 countries.

Ministry/Service

Most members of the American province minister to the young through education, from elementary to college levels. This milieu offers a variety of opportunities for ministering: teacher, administrator, counselor, librarian, campus minister, etc. Several Brothers exercise a supportive ministry as infirmarian, cook, orchardist, radio engineer, etc. Brothers also work on diocesan and parish levels. The teaching Brothers staff institutions in Maine, New York, Ohio, Massachusetts and Illinois. Home missions are found in West Virginia and Alaska. Volunteers are accepted and encouraged for the foreign missions.

Formation Program

Upon expressing a genuine interest in a Church career as a religious Brother, the qualifying individual joins the Contact Program. During these months of getting acquainted, there are occasions for visits to local communities for religious and social events and for periodic spiritual and professional counseling.

In the affiliate stage, the candidate lives in the formation center with the formation team, sharing in their life and participating in a ministry. This period of mutual evaluation lasts at least one year.

The novitiate year for the study and practice of the Brothers' *Rule of Life* serves as the formal introduction to the religious life as lived in the community with its charism and ministry inherited from the founders. Successful completion of the studies at this stage leads to the temporary profession of the vows of poverty, chastity and obedience for one year.

During the post-novitiate period of temporary profession, the Brother is given opportunities for exercising a ministry in Christian education or in an allied field and has an obligation for his ongoing professional and religious development. This stage climaxes with the perpetual profession of the vows after an experience of 5 to 9 years as a Brother in community.

Specific Information

The Brothers of Christian Instruction do have an official habit consisting of a lay suit of dark colors. The traditional cassock and lay clothing may be worn when appropriate to the situation and locale.

Any Catholic male with the following qualifications may seek admission into the Brothers' formation program:
• a desire to consecrate his life to God in imitation of Jesus while at the service of his neighbor in cooperation with the local Church
• suitable physical and mental health
• average intelligence, preferably with a college degree.

Cistercian Abbey Our Lady of Dallas

"To Be Aflame and To Enlighten Is Perfection"

History/Charism

This monastic community pursues the ideal of following Christ by living as monks, priests and teachers.

Their roots attach them to the spirituality of the Benedictine Rule and the Cistercian tradition. Founded in the last decade of the 11th century, the Cistercian Order sought to implement the ideal of St. Benedict's Rule in its original purity and authenticity. Under the spiritual leadership of St. Bernard of Clairvaux, the Cistercians became a major force in shaping medieval Europe. Their monasteries spread all over the Western world.

Ever since the 18th century, many Cistercian monasteries have combined the ideal of community life with priestly ministry and the work of education.

The ideal was transplanted to Dallas when the University of Dallas invited a group of Hungarian Cistercians to help establish a Catholic university of high academic standards in the Dallas-Fort Worth area. Shortly afterwards in 1962, the Cistercians opened a secondary school for boys. Today in grades 5-12 more than 200 boys attend the Cistercian Preparatory School built adjacent to the Abbey. The school is considered one of the leading private schools in Texas. Its graduates attend the best colleges of the country.

Ministry/Service

The Cistercians of Dallas serve as teachers and priests for their students in their own school and at the University of Dallas. Every class in the Prep School is under the direct guidance of a Cistercian form master who stays with the same class helping them form a true community.

Besides serving in the School and at the University, the Cistercians operate one parish and assist in several others.

Formation Program

A young man may get acquainted with the Cistercian community in various ways: through correspondence, periodic visits to the Abbey or through postulancy. If accepted, he will begin a one year novitiate, an intensive training in prayer life and community living. After the novitiate, he will complete his spiritual and academic training preparing him for the priesthood and teaching. Upon obtaining an undergraduate degree, he will pursue graduate studies in theology which may be followed by graduate studies in a secular teaching field.

The Abbey accepts candidates before the completion of college but not before graduation from high school. Each case is evaluated individually.

Specific Information

Unlike the Cistercians of the Strict Observance (Trappists), our Abbey is not a strictly "contemplative community." Its motto was chosen from the writings of the greatest Cistercian, St. Bernard of Clairvaux: TO BE AFLAME AND TO ENLIGHTEN IS PERFECTION. The motto declares the essential connection between spirituality and ministry, interior life and apostolic dedication, action and contemplation.

Claretians

"Special Emphasis on Service to the Disadvantaged and Often-Neglected Minorities"

History/Charism

The Claretians are neither the biggest nor the smallest religious congregation in the United States, but they do bring a special timeliness and quality to their ministries.

Since their founding in 1849, they have followed the tradition of St. Anthony Claret by striving in all their apostolic work to instill in others a lasting appreciation of the social, moral, intellectual and spiritual values that make for a rational, purposeful existence.

The involvement of Claretian priests and brothers with many of the urgent concerns of modern society—improved health care for those in economic distress, neighborhood renewal and help for culturally marginated Hispanics, for example—is possible because the individual training and community structure of the Congregation allows them to make maximum use of their own personal talents.

The Claretians function as a religious community, and in all their ministries, small teams of priests, or priests and brothers, are arranged to provide normal, attainable goals for the personal growth and development of their individual members.

Ministry/Service

As heirs to the missionary spirit of their founder, priests and brothers of the Claretian Congregation fulfill many different ministries, with special emphasis on service to the disadvantaged and often-neglected minorities in the U.S. and overseas.

They staff inner-city parishes in a number of Mexican-American and Puerto Rican Communities.

They perform missionary duties in such Third World areas as Central America and West Africa, seeking to develop lay ministers and to counteract the social evils of illiteracy, poverty and malnutrition.

As campus chaplains, they bring a Christian presence to secular colleges and universities.

They publish the most widely quoted Catholic magazine in the country, *U.S. Catholic*, as well as specialized newsletters, books and pamphlets dealing with religious and social issues of the day.

They serve as hospital and prison chaplains, preachers, teachers, and counselors, and as outspoken advocates of social justice and human advancement. Since their arrival in the U.S. in 1902, the Claretians have undertaken special ministries as the need arose, and this pattern will continue through the 1980's.

Formation Program

The Claretians invite inquiries from candidates to the priesthood or brotherhood, ages 18 through 39. Programs are available for college students, college graduates, and for older candidates.

The academic and spiritual formation of future Claretian priests and brothers includes part-time ministries which the seminarians pursue by personal choice. They may, for instance, teach in inner-city schools or help out in parishes and CCD programs. In the summer, some join Claretian missions in Mexico or Guatemala.

Most candidates for the priesthood attend the Catholic Theological Union in Chicago or the Graduate Theological Union in Berkeley, CA.

Specialized studies in a particular field at the post-graduate level are readily available for all Claretian priests and brothers.

It is part of the training that will prepare them for the day when they can put their Christian concern into full play—in a spiritual and especially practical way—for the benefit of those they serve.

Specific Information

If you wish to receive the Claretians' free newsletter, WORD ONE, for young people interested in social action and religion, send your name and address to the Claretian Vocation office.

Comboni Missionaries

"Special Love of the Poorest and Most Abandoned"

History/Charism

In the early 19th century the church became more aware of the need for evangelization in Africa. Daniel Comboni was one of those who jumped into this work heart and soul. After an expedition into southern Sudan which cost the lives of most of his companions, he returned to Rome, sure of the need, but wondering about the methods and manpower available.

In 1867 he founded a group to evangelize Africa because they were the "poorest and most abandoned" people he knew. In later years, upon the request of the Holy See, care of the poorest and most abandoned of Latin America was undertaken as well. From the beginning, members were recruited from many nations, including those areas being served. Several native orders have been founded by Comboni Missionaries, fulfilling Comboni's dream of natives becoming missionaries to their own people.

Total dedication to missionary service, recognition of all humankind as brothers and sisters, special love of the poorest and most abandoned...these were Comboni's ideals. They are the Comboni Missionaries' ideals today.

Ministry/Service

As a strictly missionary community, we serve in 33 countries of the world, fulfilling almost every imaginable apostolate. The needs of those we serve determine our work. The sacraments, religious instruction, organization of basic communities, medicine, education, agriculture, technical training, orphanages...the list goes on and on. All done to help and to witness by our lives what Christ has taught us. It's hard to imagine a skill or talent that cannot be useful in missionary work.

Formation Program

Priests: College residence programs designed to give a good Catholic education while helping the candidate mature physically, mentally, psychologically, spiritually and socially. The candidate gets to know our lifestyle and work and thoroughly examines his possible vocation.

Associate programs and vocation discernment programs on the high school and college levels achieve to a lesser degree the same goals while allowing the candidate to live at home.

The first year of theological studies is also the year of postulancy, when a candidate is asked to make a decision.

Novitiate: An eighteen-month, intensive program involving study of one's self and one's relationship with God, his people, and our congregation.

Scholasticate: Three years with temporary vows studying theology, usually done outside one's native country in one of seven scholasticates around the world.

Brothers: Similar to priests except the subjects taken in school are aimed at developing the candidate's skills in the field of his choice.

Specific Information

The Comboni Missionaries are 1800 priests and brothers from 20 countries, working in 33 countries. They make a joyful attempt to return God's love by serving the poorest and most abandoned around the world. Men of different nations live and work side by side, conscious that all peoples are children of God and therefore their brothers and sisters. Their lives are dedicated to sharing the "Good News" with them by word and action.

The Crosiers

Canons Regular of the Order of the Holy Cross

"Living the Triumph of the Cross in Ministry, Liturgy and Community"

History/Charism

We Crosiers were founded by Blessed Theodore de Celles in the year 1210. Under the Rule of St. Augustine we Crosiers find our source for prayer, ministry, and fellowship in the context of community living. The central symbol of our spirituality is the Cross of Christ.

Our official name is Canons Regular of the Order of the Holy Cross. Historically canons were clergymen who chose to live together at the cathedral parish in the service of the local bishop. The canons lived in the midst of the church as opposed to monks who "left" the world. Canons Regular take the vows of celibacy and poverty as distinct from the secular canons who take only the vow of obedience. In 1210 Blessed Theodore founded a Canons Regular group at Holy Cross Church in Clairieux, Belgium. Together the canons worked and prayed officially for the Church. In this tradition we Crosiers live the vows of poverty, celibacy and obedience and dedicate ourselves to prayer and service in the midst of the Church.

Ministry/Service

We Crosiers involve ourselves in a large variety of ministries, always in an attempt to serve the Church's current needs and according to our means. We see this variety as a sign of our flexibility and our desire to discern the Church's present needs. As such, we are involved in many types of pastoral work including the staffing of large and small parishes throughout the United States and a Ministry and Renewal Center. Many Crosiers are involved in education, staffing a high school and junior college seminary program in Onamia, Minnesota while others involve themselves in education in other high schools and colleges. We are involved in Hispanic Ministry as well as a vibrant and dynamic mission community serving the Church in Irian Jaya, Indonesia. Thus, our members teach, counsel and work in various ministries throughout the country, each according to his own gifts and talents.

Formation

Candidates for the Crosier Novitiate are accepted only after they have completed college or the equivalent in vocational training. The Crosier Pre-Novitiate Program consists of the Inquiry Stage, Contact Stage, Postulancy and, if accepted, the Novitiate Program in Hastings, Nebraska where the man spends a year of intense learning about the Crosiers and our Way of Life. It is here that the candidate makes a decision about whether or not to commit himself to the Crosier way in preparation for first vows.

From novitiate a priesthood candidate would normally join our Crosier Community in Chicago where he would attend Catholic Theological Union for studies. Brotherhood candidates will most likely move into another Crosier Community to pursue their specified interests.

We see formation continuing throughout the life of each Crosier. As a point in that total formation both brotherhood and priesthood candidates make a solemn commitment to God in the Crosier way of life. Ordination comes after solemn vows for priesthood candidates.

Specific Information

Each religious order or congregation claims certain gifts from its founder and tradition. We Crosiers claim seven such charisms arising from the vision of Blessed Theodore and nearly 775 years of tradition. These gifts, of course, are not exclusively ours, but we place special emphasis on them in our day to day living: Life Setting of Prayer, Liturgy, Community, Poverty, Hospitality, Pastoral Ministry, Cross.

We live out our vows of poverty, celibacy, and obedience in the context of community life and prayer. As religious men under the standard of the Holy Cross, we attempt to spread the good news of God's Kingdom to men and women in the world. We place special emphasis on the Cross as a medium for resurrection. We model this mystery of the Cross with our maxim "In the Cross, Salvation!" as we commit our lives to service in the Church. Our major feast day is September 14—the Triumph of the Holy Cross.

Diocesan Laborer Priests

"A Secular Institute of Priests Centered Upon Vocation"

History/Charism

The Diocesan Laborer Priests is a Secular Institute of Priests, originated in Spain in 1886, whose basic thrust is the care, promotion and sustenance of priestly and religious vocations, youth, and Christian lay leaders.

Ministry/Service

The priests of the Institute work in diocesan or interdiocesan seminaries as spiritual directors, teachers and/or administrators. Also, in their work with youth, they occupy chairs in colleges and universities, and cooperate in Newman Centers and youth organizations. Through Marriage Encounter (founded by a member of the Institute), the family, and other Christian movements, they help in the formation of the Christian lay leader. Finally, some parish work is always assumed from its members, especially through and in "vocational parishes."

Formation Program

A candidate for the Diocesan Laborer Priests is formed in a regular diocesan or interdiocesan seminary or in a house of studies of the Institute. Theoretical and practical knowledge of the Charism is always added. Before the candidate is ordained as a priest, one year of concentration or of mutual analysis takes place, yet studies are not interrupted. Once ordained, the priest remains incardinated in a diocese. There is also the option for the candidate of being ordained directly through the Institute which is of Pontifical Right.

Specific Information

The Diocesan Laborer Priests, since they are not religious, do not have a vow of poverty. They give a word of living in an exemplary, priestly way. But they have the vows of obedience and of chastity. Solid internal spirituality, serious academic preparation, life in flexible teams characterized by openness of heart, spirituality centered upon the altar and the Eucharist, and sharing in a common task are the key traits of a Diocesan Laborer Priest.

Divine Word Missionaries

"The World Is Our Parish"

History/Charism

Divine Word Missionaries is a multiracial congregation of more than 5000 Priests and Brothers, who are devoted almost exclusively to home and foreign missionary apostolates in Europe, Asia, Africa, South America and the United States. They witness to the Word of God in more than forty countries.

In one way or another, Divine Word Missionaries share Christ's dream and mission: "Go out into the whole world and make disciples of all nations." Each of us has an inner conviction that our life's calling and commitment is to that dream and vision. As Christ was sent by the Father to transform the world, so we are also sent, each in his own way.

Ministry/Service

The mission of Christ takes place in our world...where funds are needed,...where men must be prepared and tested through a process of education and formation. Christ wants us to reach out with an open hand and a warm heart to all in need, the starving, the lonely, the oppressed, the alienated, the slandered, the confused, the emotionally starved,...to everyone whom sin has touched.

Many SVDs serve the poor in cities and rural areas. Others operate schools and leprosaria. Still others publish Catholic magazines and newspapers, operate Catholic radio and TV stations, teach in universities and train future Brothers and priests. They run experimental farms, organize community development programs and serve people in Black, Hispanic, and Appalachian parishes.

Formation Program

Young men of high school age may choose to attend one of two high school seminaries in East Troy, Wisconsin or in Perrysburg, Ohio. Others begin their education at Divine Word College Seminary in Epworth, Iowa. The latter is the only Catholic mission seminary college in the U.S.

We have special programs for Hispanic seminarians at Casa Guadalupe in East Los Angeles and for Blacks at the Black House of Studies in New Orleans. The Associate Program is specially designed for other men of college age or older.

All candidates attend novitiate at Bay St. Louis, Mississippi. It's a one year course of intense spiritual and personal development. Afterwards, students for the priesthood continue their graduate work in Theology at Catholic Theological Union in Chicago, while Brothers complete their training in individualized programs adapted to their own skills and talents. Each member in temporary vows has an opportunity to spend one or two years working in the home or foreign missions.

Specific Information

Christ's call is indeed true today: "The harvest is ripe, but laborers are few..." We invite you to come and minister with us!

Order of Preachers
Dominican Fathers and Brothers

"To Give to Others the Fruits of Their Contemplation"

History/Charism

The Order of Preachers was founded in 1216 by St. Dominic de Guzman in response to a then desperate need for informed preaching—a need that could not be met by the existing resources within the Church. Against a heresy which denied the dignity of our humanity, St. Dominic trained a group of preachers who would serve the Church in its affirmation of the world as the place where Christ was discovered. He adapted the structure of monasticism so that his Friars, vowed to poverty, chastity, and obedience, were nevertheless free to move wherever their preaching was needed. He replaced the tradition of manual labor with the discipline of study, so that what was preached would be part of the Church's sustained reflection on the mystery of Christ. And he began a tradition of spirituality that is rooted in community life, liturgical and choral prayer, and meditation—a sprituality which meant to bear the fruit of an active apostolate.

Centuries ago, St. Thomas Aquinas gave to Dominicans their motto: "To give to others the fruits of their contemplation."

Ministry/Service

Dominicans continue to draw on their origins and a history of adaptation in an attempt to serve their calling: To Preach the Gospel. While the preaching apostolate remains the chief commitment of the Order, that task is supplemented by numerous other ministries. From the beginning, Friars sought association with centers of learning and teaching. Also, a variety of campus ministries continues to be a vital mission. Providence College, in Rhode Island is operated by the Order of Preachers. Our interests and activities extend to retreat centers, research hospitals, preaching teams, a number of parishes, university campus ministries, art, liturgy, communications and media, as well as ministries in areas of social justice. The Friars also staff foreign missions in Peru, Pakistan, Latin America and Africa.

Formation Program

The Eastern, Central and Southern Dominican Provinces require that clerical aspirants have completed four years of college; the Western Province asks that two years of college work be completed. If accepted, an aspirant spends a full year of novitiate in his province, during which time he seeks to determine if he is fit for religious life as a Dominican. On the completion of the novitiate year he makes the vows of poverty, chastity and obedience for a period of three to five years, and begins his formal course of studies. This will usually last for six to eight years and is comprised of such subjects as philosophy, biblical studies, systematic theology, Church history, canon law and pastoral ministry. Philosophical, theological and pastoral studies are done in ecumenical and Dominican settings in Washington, D.C., St. Louis, Missouri, and Berkeley, California.

Specific Information

Dominic envisioned a family of priests, brothers and sisters proclaiming the message of Jesus. A call to ordination is not a necessary dimension for a Dominican vocation. A man may feel called to join our preaching community as cooperator-brother. Such men, with a background in the arts and trades, commerce, the professions and academic world may find their calling to the Christian ministry fulfilled in the Order of Preachers.

The time of spiritual, academic, pastoral and professional formation seeks to bring to fruition the personal charisms of each friar as he responds to God's call within the Dominican community.

The Edmundite Fathers and Brothers

"An Unpretentious, Down-to-Earth Spirit"

History/Charism

The Society of Saint Edmund was founded in Pontigny, France, in 1843 to work for the glory of God and the salvation of neighbor through the evangelization of those who had left the faith. Today, our 100 members evangelize those who are the spiritually and materially poor in a variety of pastoral, missionary and educational apostolates in Alabama, Vermont, Connecticut, Louisiana, Michigan, Quebec, Venezuela, England, and France. We are an apostolic and clerical religious congregation of pontifical right. Our priests and brothers live the public vows of poverty, chastity and obedience. With an unpretentious, down-to-earth spirit, we strive to communicate the love of the hearts of Jesus and Mary.

Ministry/Service

Edmundite service to the Church reflects a unity in diversity. Though we are engaged in a variety of pastoral, missionary, and educational ministries, we share a common spirit and integrate and share our life and mission with those whom we serve. Those we serve recognize and admire our camaraderie, friendship, adaptability, responsiveness and hospitality.

Our pastoral and missionary work is to the Blacks and the poor in the rural South, to the English speaking Catholic minority of Canada's Quebec province, to those in rural New England, and to retreatants at our Retreat House in Mystic, Connecticut. Our educational apostolate is at Saint Michael's College in Winooski, Vermont and we assist at Xavier University in New Orleans.

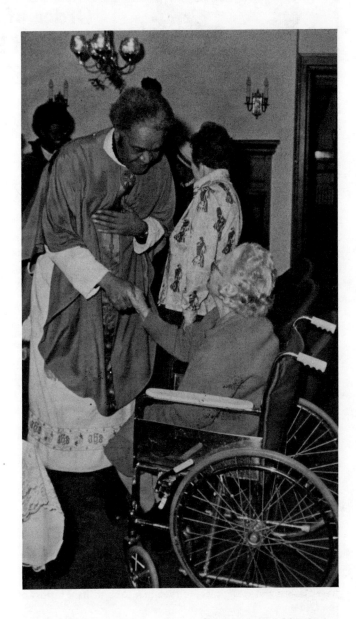

Formation Program

Since no one should enter religious life without suitable preparation, a period of association with the Society precedes admission to the Novitiate. The Pre-Novitiate program consists of two parts: a period of initial non-resident association and a period of resident postulancy. During association a variety of potential workshops, retreats and seminars are offered at convenient times. Through a resident postulancy program the candidate is led to see God's action in his life. He grows in his knowledge of the Edmundite life and mission.

Religious life in the Society of Saint Edmund begins with the Novitiate. It lasts for one year at Enders Island, Mystic, Connecticut. The principal purpose of the Novitiate is to initiate the novice into the essential and primary requirements of religious life. The Novitiate's purpose is achieved through spiritual direction; a meaningful liturgy; a study of and practice in the methods of mental prayer and celebration of the Liturgy of Hours; experience and guidance in community living; instruction in Scripture, Theology, Church History, Mariology, and religious life; and, a study of the Society's life and mission, past and present.

The Post-Novitiate academic program for priesthood candidates has two parts: college studies, leading to the bachelor's degree, and the post-college professional study at Notre Dame Seminary, New Orleans, Louisiana. Brothers in Post-Novitiate formation receive professional instruction in those sciences and arts necessary for their future work in the Society. Beyond the basic courses in Sacred Scripture, they receive courses in the fundamentals of Christian dogmatic, moral ascetical and liturgical theology.

Specific Information

Candidates must have completed at least two years of formal education beyond High School for admission to the Novitiate. For those applying as priesthood candidates, they must demonstrate an ability to pursue the necessary undergraduate and graduate studies prescribed. Normally, candidates are not considered after age 35.

Franciscans

Order of Friars Minor
Order of Friars Minor Conventual
Order of Friars Minor Capuchin

Who Was St. Francis of Assisi?

Francis was born in 1182. His was a tumultuous world torn by political, economic and spiritual crises. He was raised in a wealthy merchant family and found himself stepping on the poor. He went to war for his hometown and found himself in prison. He saw a Church in need of reform and found himself alienated. The pain Francis experienced and the pain he found himself inflicting on others left him deeply troubled. He began searching for a new way.

Francis turned to the gospel to hear its call and to receive direction. The gospel did not take him away from the struggle, the wars, the oppression and the sinful Church. Instead, it led him deep into their midst. Gradually the Lord led Francis to seek out caves for solitude and prayer, to embrace a leper and call him "brother," to live gospel poverty and penance, to plead with Christian crusaders and a mideast sultan to make peace, and to compose one of the great creation songs of all times, "The Canticle of Brother Sun."

What Are Franciscans Like Today?

St. Francis founded *three orders*: the Friars Minor (Lesser Brothers), the Poor Clares and a third order for married and single lay people.

The *Friars Minor* have always acknowledged the Rule of St. Francis as an unalterable pattern for living the gospel. Yet Francis' life was so radical and rich that no one person or group could live up to his vision. The Friars Minor split into *three different branches* during the course of history, each developing and interpreting Francis' values and rule of life. The *Order of Friars Minor,* the *Order of Friars Minor Conventual* and the *Order of Friars Minor Capuchin* emerged because two ever present tendencies have clashed and sometimes even continue to clash in the history of the Order.

Focusing on the "pure ideal," some friars interpret the Rule in the light of Francis' life and his Testament. Other friars endeavor to bring the ideal up to date with a "contemporary adaptation" in accord with the practical necessities of the Order and its apostolic works as they evolve.

In the 13th century, soon after Francis' death, the tension between these two tendencies gave rise to two groups called "Spirituals" and "the Community." By the early 14th century the extreme "Spirituals" left not only the order but also the Church. In the 15th century "the Community," then known as "Observants," stressed small group living in remote places which fostered fraternal closeness and contemplative prayer overflowing into regular preaching tours into the cities. "Conventuals" stressed monastic stability and liturgy while living in "conventos" (houses) in the cities with the people—poor and educated alike.

In 1517 Pope Leo X formalized these differences into two separate branches of the Franciscan Order—the Conventuals and the Observants (who were later named the Order of Friars Minor). A few short years later, division between "Strict Observants" and "Regular Observants" arose. In 1528 Pope Clement VII recognized the "Strict Observant" Capuchins (*capuche,* pointed hood) as legitimately living Franciscan life by stressing even more withdrawal from the world and greater austerity, simplicity, poverty and contemplation.

The drive toward the life of a hermit expressed in the Capuchin movement and the drive toward the monastic life expressed in the Conventual movement have always been present in the history of the Order. Francis himself struggled with that tension. In the end, these differences are always overcome in the Order by the essential call to be friar and minor. As Capuchin historian Fr. Lazaro Iraiarte de Aspurz notes, "Family quarrels, far from sapping the strength of the Order or lowering it in the estimation of the outside world, had given fresh stimulus to Franciscan values..."

Today, Franciscans are following the call of the Church in Vatican II by listening to the gospel, the spirit of Francis our founder and the signs of the times. Franciscan, Conventual and Capuchin brothers and priests pray and work both in the mainstream Church in parishes, schools, and hospitals, and also with the world's alienated, poor and neglected.

The *Poor Clares* are co-workers with their Franciscan brothers and sisters through a life of prayer—cloistered, poor, simple—a radical witness centered on the Lord.

Francis' *Third Order* evolved into two groups: The *Secular Franciscan Order* embraces married and single lay people joyfully changing the world by bringing the gospel to their families, their jobs and their neighborhoods. The *Third Order Regular* grew out of the Secular Order. With the passage of time, some of the penitents began living communally while continuing their works of mercy and service. In 1447 Pope Nicholas V united these groups into a worldwide order. Other Third Order sisters and brothers constitute diocesan communities under a local bishop. They were often originally organized to meet a particular local need or ministry.

Today over one million Franciscan men and women inhabit the earth. In the U.S. there are about 100,000 Franciscans: 55,000 Secular Franciscans, 40,000 sisters, and 6,000 brothers and priests. Franciscan religious communities can also be found in the Anglican and Lutheran communions.

New York Daily News columnist Dick Ryan wrote in 1981 during the 800th anniversary of Francis' birth, "I have never been around a group of people who, collectively and individually, enjoy life so much, live it simply, gentle the air they breathe and put something in the whole idea of holiness that is as human as it is filled outrageously with humor."

In the next three pages take the opportunity to discover life in the Order of Friars Minor, in the Order of Friars Minor Conventual and in the Order of Friars Minor Capuchin.

Franciscans
Order of Friars Minor

"The Lord Gave Me Brothers"

History/Charism

St. Francis of Assisi described the beginning of the religious order named after him in a direct and simple way. It was not a group of "followers" or "disciples." They were "brothers." At the end of his life, in his Testament, Francis wrote, "When God gave me some brothers, there was not one to tell me what I should do; but the Most High himself made it clear to me that I must live the life of the gospel."

The Lord has called Franciscans to live according to the gospel—not alone, but within a community of brothers. It is within and because of this community that a vocation is brought to maturity. The friars not only live side by side, striving towards the same goal and helping one another to reach it, but we turn toward one another in mutual love, according to the example and commandment of the Lord.

Franciscans try to have a balance between prayer life and apostolic work. We are not monks. Our place is out living and working with all of God's people, trying to make his love more present in the world.

Francis loved all of God's creation. He ministered with simplicity and joy and so we his brothers try to live simply—unencumbered by material concerns, and joyfully—trusting in God's care.

Ministry/Service

In the Rule of 1223 Francis gave his brothers direction for their ministry: "The friars to whom God has given the grace of working should work in a spirit of faith and devotion and avoid idleness, which is the enemy of the soul, without however extinguishing the spirit of prayer and devotion, to which every temporal consideration must be subordinate." That Franciscan spirit springs up everywhere. We do every and all kinds of work, from parishes to poverty programs, from medicine to the missions, from classrooms to communication arts. Franciscans are involved in retreat work, universities, drug programs, counseling, youth work, high schools, the aged, campus ministry, inner city work, hospital and military and institutional chaplaincies, downtown churches, urban and rural parishes, home and foreign missions, work with the oppressed and the various manual trades which serve the fraternity and the Church.

Formation Program

When pressed to formulate a rule for his brothers in 1223, Francis began "The Rule and life of the Friars Minor is this, namely, to observe the holy gospel of our Lord Jesus Christ by living in obedience, without property, and in chastity." Rule and life were the same for Francis. The gospel is the Franciscan life; the rule is simply to live the Good News.

Formation in this "rule and life" proceeds through definite steps. Candidacy helps you make the transition from life in the Church as a layman to religious community life. Novitiate is your official entrance into the Order with the opportunity to "re-found the Order" in your own heart. Temporary vows provide lived experience of Franciscan life during training for ministry as a brother or priest and leading to final vows.

Each province in the U.S. organizes and structures this formation period differently, reflecting the diverse cultural and regional characteristics that constitute the Church in the United States.

Specific Information

As you contact a friar in the province nearest you and as you search and grope for direction and decision, you may find Francis' own early prayer encouraging and helpful.

Most high, glorious God,
enlighten the darkness of my heart, and give me, Lord,
a correct faith,
a certain hope,
a perfect charity,
sense and knowledge,
so that I may carry out your holy and true command.

Franciscans
Order of Friars Minor Capuchin

"Brother to All, Especially the Poor and Lowly"

History/Charism

Francis of Assisi, often called "Everybody's Saint," has remained a curiously attractive personality since his birth almost eight hundred years ago. Pope John Paul II has described this unique man as one "who wrote Christ's Gospel in incisive characters in the hearts of the men of his time."

At the tomb of the saint the Holy Father prayed: "Help us, St. Francis of Assisi, to bring Christ closer to the Church and to the world of today....The difficult social, economic and political problems, the problems of culture and contemporary civilization, all the sufferings of the man of today, his doubts, his denials, his disorders, his tensions, his complexes, his worries....Help us to express all this in the simple and fruitful language of the Gospel. Help us to solve everything in an evangelical key, in order that Christ himself may be 'the Way—the Truth—the Life' for modern man."

The Capuchin movement began in Italy in 1528 with Father Matthew of Bascio. The desire to renew the vigor of Franciscanism led to an independent branch of the Franciscan Order, the Order of Friars Minor Capuchin. You often see the identifying initials—O.F.M. Cap.—behind a friar's name. The Capuchins came to this country in the 1630's and have been here almost continuously ever since.

Ministry/Service

Capuchin Constitutions state, "The chief apostolate of the lesser brothers is this: to live the gospel life in this world honestly, simply, and joyfully." Secondarily, the Order, seeking to transmit the Franciscan message, has through its history emphasized missionary work and preaching, but have not limited itself to any particular form of activity. Capuchin Friars, both priests and brothers, have been described as general practitioners serving the needs of the Church.

Their service today is a varied, flexible one involving many-sided activities such as: missionary outreach at home and abroad, pastoral ministry in parishes, retreats and renewal programs, health care and institutional chaplaincies, teaching, youth and family counseling, campus ministry, etc.

Formation Program

Candidates for the Capuchin Order may be accepted at almost any level of education or age.

High School: Both non-resident and resident seminary programs are available, depending on the area of the country you are in, for those working toward a high school diploma.

Postulancy: Though requirements vary from one Province (area of the country) to the other and according to the individual, a period of more formal contact with the Order is required. Resident and non-resident arrangements are used. It is a post high school program and may be done in the context of secular employment, technical training, or college studies.

Novitiate: A special year, his first as a Friar, during which the novice studies Capuchin Franciscan history, life, customs, and spirituality, prayerfully making them his own in fraternal involvement and personal growth.

After Novitiate: Temporary vows are pronounced generally for three years after which the friar may make profession for life. He then receives assignment to a fraternity and a ministry as a brother, continues academic or technical training for his work, or continues studies for the priesthood.

Specific Information

The Capuchin Order is divided into territories called Provinces, each having its own formation programs. While a man may join the Order anywhere in the world, it is suggested that he contact the vocation director of the Province nearest him.

Franciscans
Order of Friars Minor Conventual

"To Be A Living Gospel"

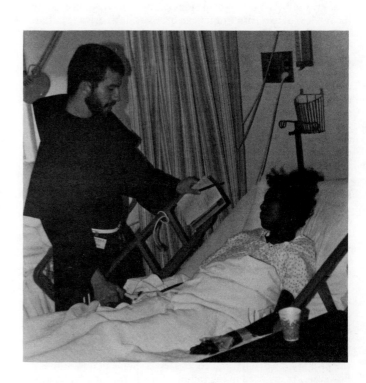

History/Charism

The Franciscan Friars within the Order of Friars Minor Conventual form one part of the Franciscan family founded by St. Francis of Assisi. All Friars share a fraternal community life of prayer and perform a variety of apostolic works. Their lifestyle is rooted in the ideals and values of the Gospel as exemplified by their founder. Some are Friar Priests and some are Friar Brothers. All, however, are brothers to each other, bound together by the fraternity of St. Francis.

Making maximum use of every personal talent, a Friar thus proclaims to the world that Christ is alive and has concern for his people. Today's Friars all strive to BE what Francis was to the world of his day, a living Gospel.

Ministry/Service

Franciscan Friars in the United States minister to the material and spiritual needs of people within parishes, high schools, colleges, hospitals, nursing homes, retreat centers and information centers. Some serve in inner-city parishes; others in campus ministries and prayer groups. These same services also reach the foreign missions staffed by the Friars in Amami Oshima, Japan, Ghana and Zambia, as well as Australia, Mexico, Honduras, Costa Rica and Brazil.

Formation Program

The personal formation of a Friar proceeds through several distinct stages. Each stage helps the Friar grow in Christian, Franciscan and personal maturity. Basic elements of Franciscan formation include a pre-Novitiate program, Novitiate and further education in areas of interest and need. Candidates for the Franciscan priesthood continue their studies at various colleges and universities. Candidates for the Franciscan Brotherhood receive training for the specialized areas of ministry. The structuring of these programs varies slightly among the American Provinces. Interested candidates are encouraged to contact the Vocation Directors in any of the provinces for further information.

Specific Information

St. Francis wishes his Friars to be both men of prayer and men of ministry among the people of God. Some of his Friars chose a life with no fixed residences and traveled from place to place. Other Friars lived by themselves. Still other Friars chose to live in towns and cities among the people they served. Within time, this latter group of Friars became known as the Conventual Franciscans. The Conventual Franciscan Friars serve throughout the United States. For specific information on the Franciscan way of life, please contact the Vocation Director nearest you!

Franciscan Brothers of Brooklyn
Religious Brothers of the Third Order Regular of Saint Francis

"My God and My All"

History/Charism

In 1858, five years after the establishment of the Diocese of Brooklyn in New York by Pope Pius IX, Bishop Loughlin engaged the services of two Irish Franciscan Brothers in his drive to initiate a Catholic School system, a vital need of the Catholic community in the 19th century. These two men, Brother Vincent Hayes and Brother John McMahon, the founders of the Franciscan Brothers in Brooklyn, arrived in the United States on May 31, 1858. For thirty-six years after this advent, the Irish Brothers continued to encourage young men to accept the challenge of an apostolate in an area of the world plagued by war, financial panic and rapid urbanization, and in a Congregation of religious beset by poverty, hardship, and all the drawbacks of a new religious community. In these early years, the Brothers established or staffed some forty schools, orphanages, camps and boarding schools in the present day New York metropolitan area. In 1873, the Brothers staffed a government-owned Indian school at St. Paul, Minnesota and opened another at Spalding, Nebraska in 1895.

The chronicles of the Congregation throughout these early years are replete with narratives of enormous sacrifice, and leave one with a sense that unreflective singlemindedness, directed precisely toward spreading the Gospel message of Jesus Christ, is the legacy of the Franciscan Brothers of Brooklyn.

Ministry/Service

Service for the Franciscan Brothers is still basically educational, for as the word denotes, we wish our service to be characterized as drawing out of persons the Christ and Christ-consciousness within. Most of our Brothers are engaged in the educational ministry on the primary, secondary and college levels. Some of our Brothers, however, are involved in the following ministries: youth ministry, campus ministry, prison ministry, communications, retreat work, special education, C.C.D., coordinators of parish religious education and other related parish ministries, diocesan officials, working with the orphaned, and hospital administration.

Formation Program

Vocation Awareness Weekend is an opportunity for Juniors in high school and older to join the Franciscan Brothers from a Friday evening to Sunday afternoon at our retreat house, St. Francis Center in Oyster Bay, Long Island, New York. These weekends are conducted two times throughout the year in November and March.

Franciscan Brothers Contact Program is a non-residential and informal association of high school graduates or older exploring the possibility of a future lifestyle as a Franciscan Brother. To achieve this end, monthly meetings are conducted in various friaries throughout the Community for prayer and discussion on the Franciscan way of life.

Franciscan Brothers Pre-Novitiate Program is a residency program opened to qualified high school graduates and older. Formal application to this program is made through the office of the Vocation Director. Upon acceptance to the pre-novitiate, the candidate or pre-novice lives in community with several Franciscan Brothers. Currently the Franciscan Brothers conduct a pre-novitiate house at Corpus Christi Friary in Woodside, Queens, New York.

Pre-novitiate formation officially begins during the Summer Orientation Program. This orientation program is conducted dur-

ing the summer months, and is an introduction to the life of the Franciscan Brother through the experience of living in community for several weeks. In addition to participation in spiritual exercises, the new candidate attends lectures and discussion groups.

While in pre-novitiate formation the candidate is expected to be self-supporting and to contribute financially to the maintenance of the pre-novitiate friary. Candidates usually pursue full time college studies or are employed at a full time job.

Franciscan Brothers Novitiate extends for a period of one full year. The purpose of the novitiate is to prepare the novice for the religious profession of the vows (poverty, chastity, and obedience). Emphasis, therefore, is given to spirituality, foundations of Franciscan life, the history of the Franciscan Brothers, a study of the *Franciscan Rule,* a study of the Franciscan Brothers *Directory* and *Constitutions*, the vows, and prayer. Apostolic experience includes volunteer work with the needy. The study of theology is also available to the novices at nearby Catholic colleges and universities in the New York metropolitan area.

Specific Information

Our Congregation is composed of Brothers (non-clerical) ministering to the needs of the People of God in dioceses of Brooklyn (including Kings and Queens counties), Rockville Centre (including Nassau and Suffolk counties on Long Island, New York), Bridgeport (Connecticut), and Saint Augustine (Florida).

Franciscan Brothers of the Holy Cross

"Engaged in Loving, Serving and Sharing"

History/Charism

The Franciscan Brothers of the Holy Cross were founded in the diocese of Trier, Germany, by Brother James Wirth, on June 12, 1862. The Chapel of the Holy Cross in the parish of Waldbreitbach on the Wied River is the origin of the Congregation. Brother James left to his Brothers the task of caring for orphans, the sick and the poor.

Ministry/Service

In the United States the Brothers are engaged in a variety of apostolic services. We teach in elementary schools, and in special education. Some of our Brothers are engaged in religious education on the parish level. Others serve in nursing, social work, skilled maintenance engineering, nursing home administration, as well as care of the mentally retarded.

Formation Program

The Franciscan Brothers of the Holy Cross accept candidates who wish to devote their service to the "sick and suffering Christ." Upon filling out the application, presenting required documents and being accepted by the Congregation, the candidate begins his initiation period into the religious community and its way of life.

The Postulant lives at our House of Novitiate. During this six month period he is introduced to the experience of community living and the apostolic endeavors of the community. He studies the foundations of religious life and Franciscan Spirituality.

After his initiation period has been completed and he has been accepted as a Brother in our Congregation, he will begin his formal training as a Franciscan Novice. The new novice is given his religious habit and for a period of two years he studies in depth the way of life he hopes to live. This program includes the study of the Franciscan Rule of Life, the history and the Constitutions of the Congregation as well as the vows in preparation for religious profession of chastity, poverty and obedience.

After Novitiate, the novice is admitted to the profession of Temporary Vows for a period of two years, followed by a further renewal period of three years. After five years of temporary profession, the Brother freely chooses to entrust his life to the Church, through the special privilege of pronouncing Perpetual Vows for his entire life.

Specific Information

The Franciscan Brothers of the Holy Cross is solely a community of Brothers. No applicant desiring to become a priest may be admitted into the Congregation.

58

Little Brothers of St. Francis

"Making Christ Present in the Ghettos, Favelos or Barrios of the World"

History/Charism

We are a contemplative community of religious Brothers, founded in 1970 in the Archdiocese of Boston by Brother James Curran, O.S.F., to live a life of contemplative prayer in gospel poverty, total self-sacrifice and prayerful solidarity with Christ's poor in the inner-city ghettos, favelos or barrios of the world. We follow the *Rule for Hermitages* of St. Francis of Assisi and our *Way-of-Life* is approved by Humberto Cardinal Medeiros. We are under the spiritual jurisdiction of the Minister General of the Order of Friars Minor in Rome.

Without formal enclosure, we embrace voluntary confinement among the poor where, in the deep center of our hearts, we foster an interior life of union with God. We strive to imitate the example of St. Francis and his early friars embracing a life of hesychastic and liturgical prayer with daily Liturgy of the Eucharist, Liturgy of the Hours, Lectio Divina, periods of silence and meditation and one hour each day of Eucharistic Adoration. Obedient to the Church, our Holy Father, the Pope, and our superiors, we are submissive to the will of God in our lives. As a means of true conversion (metanoia), we embrace chastity, humility and actual poverty, like Christ and His apostles, living in small fraternities of three or four Brothers and assuming the simple circumstances of our poor neighbors. The inner-city is the "desert" to which we withdraw in order to empty ourselves of all selfish pursuits (kenosis) and experience the authentic poverty of Christ.

We wear a Franciscan habit of common blue-denim fabric with cord and rosary. Each brother has also a pair of dungarees, a few personal items of underwear and a pair of sandals. A woolen jacket, sweater and waterproof boots are added for the winter months. We deny ourselves all other personal items and, in order to facilitate the contemplative life, we forgo television, radio, smoking and many other diversions. Our lives are filled with fraternal happiness and the joy of the Holy Spirit as our daily sustenance is provided by the Providence of God and whatever income we can earn from part-time crafts or menial jobs. We are always more than adequately provided for at the table of the Lord.

Ministry/Service

As a fruit of our contemplative prayer life, we are led to an "evangelical street ministry" to bring good news to the poor and heal the broken-hearted. We do not engage in formal institutional apostolates, but serve the Church through our contemplative presence, making Christ present by simple neighborly outreach and availability to the poor among whom we live. We encounter Jesus in the many "lepers of society" who populate our city streets. Among these "anawim" are the homeless shopping bag people, the mentally disoriented and just plain outcasts who together share a common loneliness and rejection by a materialistic and impersonal society. We seek to communicate the marvelous grace and love of God to those who need to learn how much He loves, so that they might feel His touch upon their lives. We bring the healing love of Jesus, listening to their individual problems, giving them hope and sharing with them the happiness of the gospel message. Since, we

do not aspire to professional careers, we cooperate with existing agencies and assist the needy to the hostels, soup kitchens, detox clinics and institutions that can better meet their material needs.

By returning each day to our contemplative fraternities, we are able to replenish our spirit in the love of God, Who loves the poor because they so much resemble His crucified Son. We see our vocation as "Little Brothers" to be a sign of the humility and obscurity that characterized the hidden life of Jesus at Nazareth. St. Francis exhorted his brothers: "Do not argue with unbelievers, but be humbly subject to all creatures for the love of God, and thus bear witness to what Christianity really is."

Formation Program

Qualified candidates who show a sincere desire and ability to seek the Lord Jesus in a contemplative way of life are accepted for a three to six month Observership, a six month Postulancy and a one year Novitiate before being admitted to profession. After three to six years of temporary vows, a Little Brother makes perpetual vows of Obedience, Chastity and a solemn vow of Poverty.

Specific Information

The Little Brothers of St. Francis are a non-clerical, specifically contemplative institute of Brothers *only*. Interested Catholic young men are invited, after preliminary correspondence, to apply for a week-long "Come and See" visit in order to experience our daily lifestyle and seek discernment of their call to Consecrated Life.

Third Order Regular of St. Francis of Penance

"...Let Them Live According to the Poverty, the Humility and the Holy Gospel of Our Lord Jesus Christ"

History/Charism

In preaching a life of Gospel conversion and repentance, Francis of Assisi attracted many people from all walks of life. Gradually he came to see that God was calling him to give new momentum to a movement already present among the Christian Faithful, a life of conversion—the challenge to live the Gospel in his daily life. In 1221 Francis wrote a Rule of life for those penitents living in the world. With the passing of time, some of the penitents began to live communal life, dedicating themselves to works of mercy; others began to live in remote places as hermits. In 1447 Pope Nicholas V gave these groups regular status as a religious Order and united them under a central government.

The fundamental norm of life for our friars is the following of Jesus Christ, as set forth in the Gospels, in accord with the example and teaching of St. Francis, who, by a continuous conversion to God, directed all his efforts to duplicate in his own life the likeness of the Divine Master.

Ministry/Service

Emerging from this penitential movement, Third Order Regular Franciscans today preach the Gospel message of conversion and repentance throughout the world. Our friars serve God's people in France, Germany, Spain, Italy, Sicily, Mexico, India, Yugoslavia, Africa and the United States. Many friar missionaries carry the Good News to the people of Brazil, Paraguay and Peru.

Our ministries are varied. Some of our friars are administrators, teachers, counselors in colleges, high schools and other educational institutions. Others serve in social work, religious education, parishes, health care facilities, campus ministry, rural and urban centers, home missions, and in various aspects of the ministry of reconciliation.

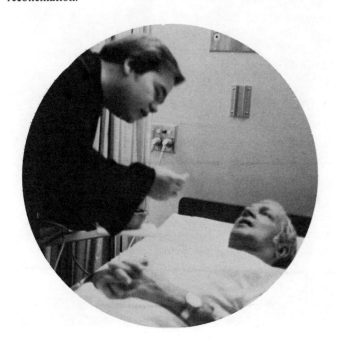

Formation Program

Pre-Novitiate: Gradual introduction to the Franciscan 'way of life' while pursuing a liberal arts education in a Franciscan formation program. College, non-college and/or professional-technical training programs available.

Novitiate: One year program providing an introduction to Franciscan fraternity, spirituality and ministry, theology of religious life and Evangelical Counsels. Profession of temporary vows at the end of this year.

Post-Novitiate: Continuation of Franciscan formation in personal development, in fraternal life, in education and in apostolic work, culmination in profession of solemn vows.

Some Specifics: The Franciscans, T.O.R. accept high school graduates, college students, college graduates as candidates both for priesthood and brotherhood.

Specific Information

What men of his own time saw in St. Francis of Assisi, the people of our time want to see in us, the Gospel of Jesus Christ alive, dynamic and challenging. The Rule and Life of the Third Order Regular says that the friars "...are to persevere in true faith and penance. We wish to live this evangelical conversion of life in a spirit of prayer, of poverty, and of humility." We "...are called to heal the wounded, to bind up those who are bruised, and to reclaim the erring."

Glenmary Home Missioners

"Serving the People of Appalachia and the Rural South"

History/Charism

The Glenmary Home Missioners were founded in 1939 to establish the Catholic Church in Appalachia and the rural South, regions heavily unchurched and with a minority of Catholics. In some areas, Catholics are as few as one-half of one percent of the population (0.5%) and people without any church identity as many as 40% to 60%.

The mission of the Glenmary brother or priest is to bring God's faithful love to His people. To do this, each missioner is trained to live and work in small town and country areas and to develop his God-given talents.

More than 100 priests and brothers of Glenmary serve in 12 states. They settle in a mission area by invitation of the Bishop and remain until a parish is firmly planted and is self-sustaining. The parish is then returned to the diocese and the missioners move on to begin anew.

Ministry/Service

Human needs of every kind confront the missioner daily. Exploitation, poverty (half of the nation's poor live in the South), substandard housing and inadequate medical service are common.

Glenmarians work with other churches and with civic groups for the benefit of all the community. They form credit unions and co-ops, organize sheltered workshops, thrift shops and centers for the retarded. They counsel alcoholics and drug addicts and people with personal problems. They serve the sick, the aged and the lonely, obtain food for the hungry, build homes for the poor and build spiritual lives of the people, Catholic or not.

Liturgies are offered and education in the Catholic Faith is given for people who have not had the opportunity to be in contact with the Church because of distance or lack of familiarity with the faith.

The Gospel is brought to people through radio, TV, newspaper and personal visitation.

Formation Program

An applicant to Glenmary must be a high school graduate. Training at the college level is conducted at the University of Dayton (Ohio) and seminarians pursue their studies at Washington Theological Union. Students spend the summers of their training period in the missions, gaining first-hand experience. In both Dayton and Washington, Glenmary students have their own residence and are directed in their formation by a Glenmary priest and/or Brother.

Brothers of Holy Cross

"At the Disposal of God and Neighbor"

History/Charism

Founded to teach in the primary schools of France after the French Revolution, the Brothers of Holy Cross originated as the Brothers of St. Joseph. The order quickly grew and then merged in 1838 with a small group of priests to form the Congregation of Holy Cross. Unique among religious communities of men, the Congregation has a society of Brothers and a society of clerics, each with its own provinces but joined by common constitutions and leadership team in Rome. The Brothers came to the United States in the early 1840's and settled first in Indiana to help establish the University of Notre Dame and then in New Orleans to establish an orphanage. Since those early beginnings in 1842, the American branch numbers over 1,200 Brothers. Since those early days, diversity has marked the Brothers' contribution to the American Church, whether it was opening the first classical high school operated by Brothers in the United States or staffing the Notre Dame Post Office since its inception. International in character, Brothers from the United States live and work in Bangladesh, Brazil, Uganda, Tanzania, Liberia, Ghana, Italy, Canada, and Mexico. True to our origins, we continue to try to live the Gospel message through an integrated life of prayer, service and community. As the Congregation's constitutions state, "In all our endeavors, pastoral and secular, we must be educators in the faith. We labor for the coming of the Kingdom of God and the building up of the world of man by striving to imbue contemporary civilization with the Christian Spirit."

Ministry/Service

Throughout the United States Brothers are engaged in a variety of ministries. Education on all levels—university, junior college, high school, middle school, religious education and special education—constitutes a strong emphasis. Likewise, Brothers engaged in social work can be found in centers for juvenile offenders, state hospitals, clinics, and parish and private counseling centers. Some of the other ministries Brothers are engaged in are: health care, youth ministry, overseas development, work with the elderly, parish and hospital ministry, farming and a variety of trades.

Formation Program

To quote the Constitutions of the Congregations, "The aim of the initial years is to assist each one to become a convinced Christian and a generous religious, mature and educated person, and a competent apostle. The program is organized in a way that permits the candidate to assume responsibility for his formation and at the same time allows him and the community to judge the reality of his vocation and his aptitude for life in Holy Cross." People are accepted into Holy Cross at the completion of high school and participate in a candidacy program for one or two years prior to novitiate. Once novitiate is finished and one's professional preparation is complete, he begins his life of ministry. Temporary vows are made after novitiate for a period of no longer than nine years.

Specific Information

Throughout our history, the diversity of lifestyles and ministry has enabled the Brothers to freely respond to the pressing needs of the culture and the Church. Traditionally enjoying this freedom, the Brothers are able to respond to the needs of the poor, oppressed, aged, unchurched and illiterate.

Priests of Holy Cross

"Men of Service to God and Neighbor"

History/Charism

Holy Cross had its beginnings during the troubled period following the French Revolution. Starting in 1835, Basil Anthony Moreau, a priest of the diocese of LeMans, France, gathered a community to live as disciples of the Lord, supporting one another in faith and being actively involved in building up God's kingdom. Our commitment in Holy Cross is for our fellow Christians an invitation to fulfill their vocations, and for ourselves it is a concrete way of working with them for the development of human society and the spread of the Gospel. From France we as a congregation have expanded to North and South America, Asia and Africa. The Constitutions of our community state our objectives:

As men dedicated to the mission of the Savior, we announce His word and labor for the establishment of His Kingdom. As Christians living in community, we seek to achieve that union in love which Christ willed for His disciples and which bound the earliest Christians together. As followers of Christ, who lived constantly in the presence of the Father, we wish to be men of prayer. As religious who vow celibacy, poverty, and obedience, we want to place ourselves completely at the disposal of God and our neighbor.

Ministry/Service

Men of Holy Cross are called to serve in a variety of apostolates. The common vocation is to make ourselves available to the service of God and neighbor. We do this through pastoral, educational and missionary apostolates. As priests we serve on parish ministry teams, as chaplains in hospitals, prisons and the military, in inner city parishes and work with migrants. In this country we staff various schools including the Universities of Portland and Notre Dame, as well as Stonehill and King's Colleges. We are involved not only in teaching and administration, but also in campus ministry and counseling. Our missions are in Africa, South America and Asia.

Formation Program

Men come to us after high school, during and after college, or after a few years in a career. Our college level program involves living with Holy Cross men. There are also contact programs for those interested in Holy Cross but attending a college without Holy Cross personnel. Men who come to us after college usually live with us for a year before going to the Novitiate.

The Novitiate is a year set apart to help a man better learn how to pray, to see more clearly the way the Lord is calling him, to learn about religious life and Holy Cross, and to decide whether the Lord is calling him. After Novitiate, men ordinarily go to the University of Notre Dame to continue their preparation for active ministry.

Specific Information

In the United States there are three Provinces of Holy Cross. An individual is free to choose whichever one he desires. However, normally the choice is made by geographic location. Each Province emphasizes a particular charism which corresponds to the goals of our founder. In Holy Cross we value the individual gifts of each man because it is through these gifts that he enriches our community and is able to detect and fulfill the demands of the Gospel today. Our men are more important than our institutions. For this reason Holy Cross is especially proud of the wide variety of works to which our priests have been called within our family.

Missionaries of the Holy Family

"Servants of God—Builders of Family"

History/Charism

The congregation of the Missionaries of the Holy Family was founded in 1895 at Grave, Holland by Fr. John Berthier. Fr. Berthier dedicated the community to the Holy Family which is "the perfect model of every religious community and of every Christian family." Fr. Berthier taught us to seek out and encourage vocations, particularly among mature adults (18-50) and the poor, and to form community by living as a family. Our community strives to live a missionary spirit by bringing the Gospel message to areas and places where others were not present or would not go.

Ministry/Service

As Missionaries of the Holy Family, we involve ourselves in a large variety of apostolates, always in an attempt to serve the Church's current needs. Throughout the world we promote and serve the needs of Church, local community, family and congregation.

Here in the North-American Province (Canada, United States, Mexico) we are involved in many types of pastoral service. As priests and brothers we work in parishes, schools, hospitals, and homes for the aged. Our work reflects the concern and respect we have for family life. Our seminary is located in St. Louis, Missouri and we staff a house of studies in Ottawa, Canada. Presently, there are fourteen students in various stages of formation.

Formation Program

Candidacy: This period is a time for the candidate and the community to become acquainted. The candidate lives our community lifestyle and participates in the formation program with the goal of entering the Novitiate.

Novitiate: This is a period of one year before vows which is set aside for intense involvement in prayer, personal growth and community living.

Post-Novitiate: Newly professed return to their house of studies for continuation of their college degree or theological studies leading to final profession and/or ordination.

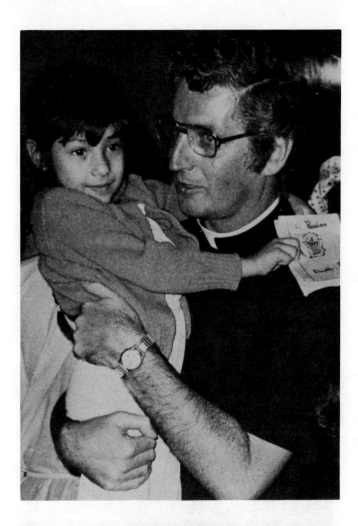

Hospitaller Brothers of St. John of God

"Participating in the Redemptive Suffering of Christ"

History/Charism

St. John of God, a man who knew love, converted from the quiet life of a shepherd and plundering soldier. People thought him a mad man, because, struck by the words of a sermon, he desired to repent for the sins of his past. Renewed and restored by his contemplation of the Passion of Christ he learned to love and began to embrace the sick, the lonely, the outcast, the sinner, and the abandoned.

He opened a small hospital where he restored all to the health of human dignity as adopted sons and daughters of God, always instructing them to return good for the evil done to them: "Remember our Lord, Jesus Christ, and His blessed Passion, and how He returned good for the evil they did to Him."

The saint was a man of great hospitality from which the word hospital takes both its name and its spirit. So captivating was the idea of hospitals, as John of God founded them and so widespread the need, that shortly thereafter his Brothers began hospitals all over the world.

The Hospitaller life seeks a mutual love and understanding with those who suffer. Through a special vow, we promise to God our Father that we will follow His Son as He spent himself on suffering humanity, in order to restore human dignity, particularly to the sick, aged, mentally, physically, and emotionally handicapped.

The Hospitaller life is a life of Brotherhood; the Brother of St. John of God learns through prayer that God abides in him and he in God.

Ministry/Service

We are "brother" to the sick and abandoned. The spirit of our founder moves us beyond the professionally trained roles in which we serve the sick, to a deeper level of ministry. Entering into the lives of those who are sick and suffering "is a sign of communion that enriches both those who receive it and those who offer it." (John Paul II to our Brothers)

This is reflected in our 39 year history in Southern California. We began with the running of soup kitchens for the elderly. The needs of Health Care for the elderly have led us into residential and skilled nursing care. The Brothers also provide spiritual, medical, surgical and preventative health care in the High Desert of San Bernardino County, and a day school and training center for the mentally handicapped child in New Jersey.

Formation Program

Our religious formation is a lifelong adventure of growing together as brothers in the spirit of our founder, St. John of God. It is one continuous process which leads a brother from the desire "to belong," towards entrance into the community and life long commitment as a Brother of St. John of God.

In the Postulant year, the candidate further evaluates his desire to belong to the community through community living, prayer, study, and direct contact with the sick. This is continued through the two years of Novitiate with further study into the spirituality and traditions of the Order. The period of temporary commitment follows for the next 6 to 9 years, with continued religious and professional studies, spiritual and community direction. After final commitment of vows the ongoing formation and struggle to grow in brotherhood in the spirit of our founder continues.

Specific Information

The life of the Brother of St. John of God is a unique gift in the Church. It is a life of union with those who suffer in a world of modern technology that denies pain and suffering. Our special vow of Hospitality unites us with the suffering of the sick which is redemptive and salvific.

Our response to the call of the Church to renew ourselves as an Order has led us to an interior search for a deeper meaning of our life, and more intimate union with our brothers and our God.

Jesuits: The Society of Jesus

"Promotion of Faith and the Service of Justice from Inner-city Classrooms to the Pacific's Outer Islands"

History/Charism

"The Jesuit vocation is essentially a call to commit one's self to Christ and His work of redemption -- a commitment in companionship with Christ, a commitment in fraternity, and always, always, always this nuance: for the greater service of God and good of souls, with everything that this implies of inner freedom, fidelity to the Spirit, complete availability, perfect mobility. It means going directly and radically to the Gospel and—there's the rub—to live its message fully, generously in the historic moment, perhaps even heroically. It is not an easy life. It is a wonderful vocation. Everything for the greater glory of God; more is not possible." (Pedro Arrupe, S.J.)

"...A Jesuit's life is rooted in the experience of God who, through Jesus Christ and in the Church, calls us, unites us to one another, and sends us forth. The Eucharist is the privileged place where we celebrate this reality. Only to the extent that he is united to God so that he be 'led gladly by the divine hand,' is a Jesuit a man on a mission. In this way, he will learn to find God in all things, the God who is present in this world and in its struggle between good and evil, between faith and unbelief, between the yearning for justice and peace and the growing reality of injustice and strife." (The 33rd General Congregation)

Ministry/Service

For over 400 years Jesuits have been fighting for Faith and Justice in various ways. They are working in such diverse apostolates as: the mission and overseas ministry; high school, college and university teaching; counseling, theological reflection, research, social and prophetic ministry; retreat and parish service; communications, hospital, military and prison chaplaincy and other special services.

Formation Program

Formal training may begin anytime after high school graduation and continue for from eight to fifteen years. A man begins his training with a two year novitiate during which he lives community life and learns the traditions and expectations of the Society of Jesus through prayer, instruction and assisting in appropriate ministerial work for the disadvantaged. At the end of his novitiate the candidate pronounces the perpetual vows of poverty, chastity and obedience. The Jesuit *brother* begins technical training. The Jesuit who is a candidate for the *priesthood,* called a "scholastic," begins his philosphical studies if he has a bachelor's degree. After philosophy, the scholastic collaborates in an active Jesuit ministry for two or three years. Following this period, known as "regency," the scholastic starts his four year study of theology, with ordination at the end of third year. "Tertianship," a period of prayer, study, guidance and ministry, precedes the final vows for Jesuit priests and brothers. This period of renewal is the last phase of the usual formation program in which the Jesuit acquires a personal dedication to Christ.

Specific Information

What is needed to become a Jesuit? Desire and ability. Our present apostolates are many and varied; our future apostolates depend upon a creative response to the needs of the world. Thus we look to develop the individual and all his gifts, inviting men who will grow responsive to the promptings of the Holy Spirit. The qualities needed include a certain spiritual and emotional maturity, intellectual competence, physical health and, most of all, a spirit of generosity. St. Ignatius asks us to pray for generosity that we might give and not count the cost, labor and not ask for any reward except the joy of knowing we are doing God's will. This giving is a service which seeks, with God's grace, to establish in others a relationship with God that will allow them to become more effective instruments for building the Kingdom.

Congregation of Saint Joseph
Fathers and Brothers of St. Joseph

"Active in Youth Ministry to Those Most in Need of Love"

History/Charism

The Congregation of St. Joseph was born in the midst of great changes in society and in the Church. The Industrial Revolution and the emergence of Italy as a nation-state were causing serious social problems in Turin, Italy. A young priest, Leonard Murialdo, saw the need to offer new solutions for new problems. In collaboration with John Bosco, Father Murialdo worked with boys and young men who were at the fringes of society. He provided food and shelter, taught religion and the vocational skills needed for meaningful employment, and helped organize young workers. There are many "firsts" among his accomplishments including the first circulating library in the area, a night school for workers and the first Catholic labor newspaper, "The Voice of the Worker." Gradually, Father Leonard's attention became focused more and more on the education of youth—inside and outside of the classroom. On March 19, 1873, he founded the Congregation of St. Joseph to carry on his work with the poor after his death. Pope Paul VI canonized him on May 3, 1970.

Ministry/Service

Today, we Fathers and Brothers of St. Joseph are committed to youth ministry in schools, parishes, missions and related areas. We are in the second year of a six year mandate from the General Chapter to work ever more concretely with the truly poor and marginated youth. Pope John Paul II described our vocation well in his exhortation given on the occasion of the 150th anniversary of the Founder's birth: "Commit your lives completely to edifying, to forming children and young people, to behaving in such a way that your life will be a continual example of virtue for them. It is necessary to become a child with children and everything to everyone in order to win all to Christ!"

Whether teaching, coaching sports, preaching, counseling or just being with youth, we try to help each person realize the immense love which God has for him/her personally, right here and now. Prayer and community life are key elements in our very active schedules. Following the Founder's motto, "Fare e Tacere," "Be Quiet and Do," we Fathers and Brothers of St. Joseph concern ourselves with actual service and not with idle debate.

Formation Program

Candidates are accepted after high school graduation. Non-resident candidates live on their own and spend a weekend with one of our local communities at least every three months. Resident candidates live in one of our houses. Both resident and non-resident candidates are given some formation in spirituality and our tradition within the community and participate as much as possible in the local diocesan formation program with candidates of other religious Congregations. All candidates must reside in one of our communities for a period of orientation for a minimum of six months before the novitiate. The novitiate lasts one full year and ends with the profession of the vows, which are renewed annually for at least four and no more than eight times before perpetual profession. After the novitiate, the new member resumes undergraduate studies if necessary. Before starting theology, an internship or practicum is done in one of our communities.

Brothers are requested to study some theology and philosophy. The full course of theology is also open to them. Religious formation is identical for candidates to the priesthood and the brotherhood.

Specific Information

A cherished feature of our Congregation's tradition is a "family style" approach to ministry and community life. From the beginning, the active cooperation of the laity has been strongly encouraged in the Josephan educational community.

Josephite Fathers and Brothers

"Dedicated Totally to Service in the Black Community"

History/Charism

The Josephites are an American Society of priests and brothers who, since 1871, have dedicated themselves to fulfilling the mission of Jesus Christ in service to the spiritual, social and educational needs of Black Americans. The Society of St. Joseph of the Sacred Heart has its roots deep in the struggle of a proud Black America for freedom from the days of the aftermath of the American Civil War. Today, the Society is the only community of religious men in the American Catholic Church dedicated totally to service of God through the Black Community. The Society is an interracial community of priests and brothers aiding one another in achieving goals through the mutual charity of community life. The Josephites respond to their mandate of evangelization by preaching Christ and love. They seek to avoid attitudes and actions of paternalism and dominance, and seek to provide a system of spiritual and psychological support. The Josephites work with total dedication and uncompromising honor in sharing with Black people the elimination of the unjust causes of social blight which are an obstacle to evangelization and the attainment of personal fulfillment in Christ.

Ministry/Service

The Josephites serve in 80 rural and inner city parishes and special ministries. The Josephites have College Campus Chaplaincies (Newman) and also serve as hospital chaplains. The Society operates a high school, college house of studies, novitiate, major seminary, neighborhood centers, a spiritual life center, and missions in the Bahama Islands. Here in the U.S., the Josephites serve in the Archdioceses of Baltimore, MD, Washington, DC, New Orleans, LA, Los Angeles, CA, Mobile, AL, and Miami, FL. Additionally the Josephites serve in the Dioceses of Wilmington, DE, Arlington, VA, Baton-Rouge, Lafayette and Lake Charles, LA, Beaumont, Dallas-Fort Worth, Galveston-Houston, and Corpus Christi, TX, Birmingham, AL, Jackson and Biloxi, MS, and St. Augustine, FL.

Formation Program

Applicants, who have graduated from high school, begin their formation program at the Josephite House of Studies in New Orleans, LA. They attend Xavier University. Applicants with degrees do a one year pre-novitiate program at this same place. Once the course of study has been completed in New Orleans, the candidates take a one year novitiate in Clayton, DE. During this year the novices strive for deeper spirituality and greater sensitivity to the workings of God's grace. Following novitiate, the candidates are professed as temporary members of the Society of St. Joseph and continue their training at St. Joseph's Seminary in Washington, DC. They pursue their theological studies at the Washington Cluster of Theology Schools and other institutions in the area.

Specific Information

The Josephites invite single Catholic men of all races to consider involvement in a vital ministry of service, as a priest or brother, to the Black community. The basic requirements for admission include good health, under 50 years of age, a high school diploma and the ability to do college work, a religious spirit and motivation to consecrate oneself to God through service to the Black community.

The LaSalette Missionaries

Modern Men, Dedicated to Mary the Mother of God,
Invite You to Share Your Life Ministering to the People of God.

History/Charism

The Missionaries of Our Lady of LaSalette came into being as a direct result of Mary's pleas to proclaim the Good News of Reconciliation. Throughout the message she communicated to two children on September 19, 1846, Mary insisted that what our day and age needed above all was a deep conversion—a reconciliation between God and and His people. Her prayer has become our password: "Do not be afraid...Make it known to all my people."

Since 1852 when the Bishop of Grenoble (France) created a body of missionaries to carry out the work of reconciliation, they have strived as priests and brothers to spread the Good News of God's healing wherever they were sent throughout the world, even behind the Iron Curtain.

Ministry/Service

Caring for pilgrims was the very first ministry undertaken by the LaSalette Community. Our Lady's appearance in France in 1846 drew large crowds that needed services of a community. Since that time LaSalettes have always dedicated shrine areas to Our Lady of LaSalette and these areas have always drawn throngs who come to hear Our Lady's message of reconciliation.

Their work is not restricted to that one area alone, however. Their men are involved in preaching ministries in pastoral centers and parishes, in schools and chaplaincies, in mass media and basic evangelization. Also, remaining true to the title "missionary", LaSalette priests and brothers have exercised their work of reconciliation in Africa, Asia, Europe, South America, as well as in home missions in North America.

Formation Program

Before Novitiate: The College Live-in Programs provide a candidate with the opportunity to experience community life with other young men who are also considering religious life/priesthood, while living at a LaSalette Community House. The candidate pursues his college degree in the field of Liberal Arts with a primary emphasis on studies in philosophy, as well as psychology, social studies, or some other approved major.

Novitiate: Novitiate is a one year program which seeks to give the candidate an understanding of religious life, the vows, and how he as a LaSalette lives out this call to community. The novitiate is located in Washington, D.C.

After Novitiate: After Novitiate, and upon religious profession, those who choose to pursue their studies to the priesthood enter a graduate studies program in theology where they prepare experientially as well as academically for ordination to the priesthood. Those who choose the vocation to missionary brother also continue on-going development of the whole person: the intellectual, the spiritual and the personal skills and talents needed for the ministry and community life of the LaSalette Missionaries.

Specific Information

The LaSalette Missionaries' ministerial objective remains flexible since they have long perceived their role as one dealing with the greatest contemporary ills. The on-going discernment of these needs constantly leads them to reflect on the signs of the times, to evaluate their capacity for response, and to move boldly into new areas of work when the Lord calls them forth.

Marianists

"Working as a Team To Build Christian Communities"

History/Charism

"Isn't there something more we can do with our lives?" When a group of very committed young people put that question to Father William Joseph Chaminade, it was the birth of the Marianists. The place was France. The time was the early nineteenth century, just after the French Revolution. The revolution's thrust for equality found expression in the spirit of this new religious order: total equality of all members—brothers and priests—and close collaboration with lay people in building Christian communities. We Marianists are proud of this heritage and people who know us are attracted by our spirit.

Community life, team ministry, and development of and collaboration with lay leadership are key elements in our spirit too. It all gets expressed like this: Whatever we do, we do together! Both in our life together and in our work we find inspiration in Mary's deep faith and openness to the spirit of the Lord. That's why we call ourselves Marianists.

Ministry/Service

On six continents around the world, we're involved in just about every kind of ministry: from high schools, universities and parishes, to the missions, care of neglected boys, retreat centers, and family renewal. There's also campus ministry, encounter movement, Christian Life Community, and adult education. Marianists are also involved in administrative work and a host of manual and technical skills too.

Formation Program

Wondering what more you can do with your life? Why not give Marianist life a closer look?

Live-in: Contact us and we'll arrange for you to spend several days or a weekend with a Marianist community near you. This way you'll have a chance to know us better. There are Marianist Communities in: California, Connecticut, Florida, Hawaii, Illinois, Maryland, Michigan, Missouri, Nebraska, New Jersey, New York, Ohio, Pennsylvania, Puerto Rico, Tennessee, Texas, Washington, Wisconsin, Canada and Mexico.

Pre-Novitiate: Sometime after the live-in experience, you might decide to apply for our Associate or Aspirancy Program. This may come during college years or after, and involves living full-time with a Marianist Community.

Novitiate: The one or two year novitiate program is the immediate preparation for professing your vows of poverty, chastity, and obedience as a Marianist. This step happens during or after college years, when you're ready for it.

Post-Novitiate: After the novitiate year, you'll prepare more directly for your future ministry. Academic preparation is tailored to individual needs and gifts. Annual vows lead to the profession of perpetual vows. If you are preparing for ordained ministry the final years of theology are after perpetual profession.

Marianphill Missionaries

"To Reach Out to People of All Races and Cultures and Bring the Good News of Salvation"

History/Charism

The Congregation of Missionaries of Marianphill began its apostolate in South Africa under the direction of its zealous founder, Father Francis Pfanner, and the inspiration of the ancient Benedictine motto: "Ora et Labora—Pray and Work."

Although Marianphill began as a Trappist monastery, it became the center of the missionaries of Marianphill which became a separate congregation in 1909 shortly after the death of Abbot Francis.

From its very inception, even when it was still a Trappist monastery, young men who came to Marianphill were quickly trained as missionaries. The monks taught by example working side by side with the native Bantu and Zulu people.

Ministry/Service

The task of Marianphill, as stated in the Constitutions, is to share the missionary task of the Church in a special way: "To cooperate in announcing the Gospel, especially to those nations who do not yet believe in Christ; to help establish and build local churches; to keep alive and deepen among the faithful a sense of responsibility for the whole Church; to solicit mission vocations and spiritually and materially support the missionary work."

Our aim is to reach out to people of all races and cultures and to bring the Good News of salvation to them. The task of the missionary is to build the Kingdom of Christ in their nation and culture, to bring the native people to positions of service and eventual leadership in the local churches.

Although the members of the Congregation may have different tasks and services, they are living the missionary vocation by cooperating in the fulfillment of the Congregation's mandate.

Today the main mission fields of Marianphill are still in Africa: Zimbabwe, South Africa, and the Transkei. Marianphill has also extended itself to New Guinea and recently to Brazil.

Formation Program

For the priesthood candidate, a college degree is acquired at St. Meinrad Seminary in Indiana. If the prospective candidate already has a college degree, he will spend one year at St. Meinrad in the pre-theology program, if the degree was not acquired at a seminary college. Before studying theology, the candidate for priesthood will spend one year in the novitiate to absorb the spirit of Marianphill and to become familiar with the life of a religious. He prepares himself to take temporary vows of poverty, chastity and obedience. The novitiate house is located in Center Valley, PA. Theological studies are completed at St. Meinrad Seminary.

A person interested in brotherhood should have at least a high school diploma. Once a brotherhood applicant is accepted, he then enters the first stage of formation, i.e., the period of candidacy. During this time, the brotherhood candidate is required to have contact with the community at least once a month. Following candidacy is a period of pre-novitiate. Upon acceptance to this stage one begins a period of discernment while living with the Marianphill community. After completion of this stage novitiate begins. Novitiate lasts for a period of at least one year. As a novice, one will examine the aspects of religious life, delve into the history and reality of the Congregation of Marianphill, and be afforded the time for intensive spiritual growth. Further training in one's occupational work will continue after novitiate, and one will be adjusted to one's talents and needs. Upon completion of training, the brother will begin his work for Marianphill.

Specific Information

Marianphill will also consider late vocations which will be accepted on an individual basis.

Marians of the Immaculate Conception

"To Serve Christ and the Church"

History/Charism

The priests and brothers of the Marian community seek to respond to Christ and His Church through continual openness to the spirit of God. Animated by this renewal, they serve God's people in varied apostolates.

This form of Marian life began in the late 17th century when Stanislaus of Jesus and Mary Papczynski founded the community under the title of the Immaculate Conception and with the intention of serving the Church with a responsive "yes" to Christ as Mary did. The changing political situation in eastern Europe in the early 1900's decimated the congregation's numbers. Extinction appeared imminent until Fr. George Matulaitis revitalized the group into today's organization, dedicated anew to serve Christ and the Church.

Ministry/Service

The Marians endeavor to let each man work for the church in the area in which he excels. Currently in the United States, the Marian priests and brothers serve God's people in parish ministry, high school teaching, preaching missions and retreats and through the printed word the Marians are also involved in missionary activity in Brazil, Argentina, Portugal and Africa.

Formation Program

Individuals who are seriously thinking of entering the Marians after discerning their vocation with the Vocation Department are admitted to our family style community of priests and brothers.

A high school graduate may determine whether he has a call to our Marian way of life through a non-resident contact program with the Vocation Department. Before one enters the community at least two years of college for the priesthood candidate and/or some work experience for the candidate to the brotherhood is required. A candidate then enters the postulancy program. Postulancy is a time for developing one's vocation, and a gradual preparation for entrance into the Novitiate. Upon acceptance into the Novitiate, the novice studies, meditates and lives Marian life in response to his call to Christ. While becoming more aware of his unique vocation, the novice deepens his personal response to Christ with the intent of embracing the Marian way of life by professing the vows of poverty, chastity, and obedience at the end of his Novitiate. During the Novitiate period, the novice not only comes to know himself, Christ, and the Congregation, but lives out the experiences gained by working with his brother Marians in apostolates away from the Novitiate. Following the Novitiate the candidate becomes a vowed member of the Congregation and for six months will then be involved in a program where he will be able to either do some apostolic work in the community or prepare himself to resume his academic or professional studies. After the Post-Novitiate experience the candidate for the priesthood resumes his studies until they are completed.

Individuals who wish to serve the Congregation in the Brotherhood have the same opportunities for continuing education and professional skills as do priesthood candidates.

Upon completion of theology the Marian is ordained priest to serve the people of God in varied ministries. Though formal training of a Marian may cease, the development of his total person is a continual process.

Specific Information

The call to life with Christ as conceived by Stanislaus and George beckons the individual to a personal relationship with Christ in the Father, and with Him as the center of one's life, to bring others to that love by all means. This personal call to live with Jesus is a gift of the Father which is sustained only by honestly cooperating with the Holy Spirit in one's daily life.

The Marians seek to respond to this gift of God, by searching through the Gospel; striving to understand, love and imitate Jesus and then bring Him to others. As followers of Jesus the members have Mary as the perfect model of love and openness to the Lord; the one who continually responded "yes" to the movements of the Holy Spirit by responding to His will. Daily the Marians strive to bring this goal into their own lives with new courage, inspiration and sometimes suffering as they search for ways of best serving Christ and the Church.

In their search for serving the Lord and His people, the Marians are not rigid in the ministries they undertake. Open to new ministries they attempt to serve in those apostolates that will bring Christ to more people, when the need is greatest and more urgent, and finally to those apostolates that would otherwise be neglected.

The Marist Brothers of the Schools

"Devoted to the Care and Education of Youth"

History/Charism

The Marist Brothers, a worldwide community of Brothers, were founded in 1817 by Blessed Marcellen Champagnat. His origins were rustic and simple coming from the fields with the strength of the plow in his arms, the fire of a simple Christian faith in his heart, and the power of a holy purpose in his will.

Once directed to the priesthood, Champagnat studied with determination and singlemindedness. During his seminary years he made friends with men of similar mold, Jean Claude Colin and John Vianney. Together with other seminarians, they founded the Society of Mary. Champagnat then became curate of a small village in the Diocese of Lyons. On one of his many trips to isolated homes, he found a dying young man ignorant of the elementary truths of faith. The memory of this experience haunted him for days; he knew he had to act. He set out to begin a community of religious men whose task would be to educate youth. This reality was quickly realized with two young men accepting the challenge to begin this venture. In the 163 years since these two people climbed the steps of that first little community, the Order's growth has been world-wide to 7800 Marist Brothers. Today, these Brothers teach on every level of education, working with youth in sixty countries on six continents.

Ministry/Service

In the United States alone there are some 400 Marist Brothers involved in administration and teaching (mostly in high schools as well as grammar schools and college), counseling, religious education coordination, retreat work, campus ministry, social work and youth rehabilitation.

Formation Program

A person, sensitive to the movement of the Spirit within his life, who wishes to discern a vocation to Marist life may join the Contact Program. This program offers a college-age person an opportunity to learn more about the Brothers through days of recollection, annual workshops and summer live-in apostolic experiences. Upon college graduation this individual would become a candidate and would live and work with the Brothers for two or more years. He would then move to the novitiate to continue his Marist training. Working closely with the Director of Novices, a young man draws closer to the time when he will publicly vow himself to poverty, chastity and obedience, assuming the role of Brother to his fellow religious and to the wider Christian community.

Specific Information

The Marist Brothers, in attempting to develop the prayer of their founder, "Unless the Lord builds the house, they labor in vain who build it," continue to strive to fulfill the mission of the Church in proclaiming the Gospel of Jesus to all men and women. The Marist Brothers can be found all over the country from New England to Texas, from Miami to Oregon, living in large and small communities. The vision of Champagnat lives on.

The Society of Mary
(Marist Fathers and Brothers)

"To Capture Mary's Spirit in Personal Living, in Mission"

History/Charism

Marists believe that the best response to the needs of people is faithfulness to the spirit and zeal of the early Christians. That first small group of Jesus' disciples, inspired by the gentle and unassuming presence of Mary in their midst, was filled with love, moved by great prayer, and was able to transform the world around them (Acts 1:12-14).

Father Jean-Claude Colin, who founded the Society in 1815, believed that Marists would strive to incorporate the very spirit of Mary into their daily lives and into their approach to the apostolate. Although hidden and unknown in the midst of the early Church, Mary was the first to welcome and share the Good News of her Son.

A Marist should be like an anonymous apostle, Father Colin stressed, one who conveys the Word of God in a gentle and quiet manner and then yields his or her position to another as the work of Christ and needs of others demand.

In a world where advancement, position and power are often the ingredients of success for its own sake, the Marist spirit invites people to ground themselves in our Lord and their idea of success in working and living for the building of his Kingdom.

Ministry/Service

From the earliest days Marists have been engaged in ministry that has responded to the demands of the Church and the needs of people. Members can be found establishing and renewing rural and urban parishes, initiating indigenous Churches (especially in the South Pacific), teaching in the high school and college classroom, serving as chaplains in colleges, hospitals, etc. The ministry of each Marist is important, but ultimately the most important dimension remains the spirit, the attitude in which it is done: gently, without calling attention to oneself.

The Marist Fathers and Brothers are members of the larger Marist Family which includes the Marist Brothers of the Schools, Marist Sisters, Marist Missionary Sisters, and the Third Order of Mary. Marists continue today to enter new apostolates as they endeavor to remain faithful to Fr. Colin who wanted them to always reach out to the "most alienated, straying and abandoned."

Formation Program

The programs of the three American Provinces differ in their offerings. Following are a general range of possibilities. College residency programs allow candidates to experience Marist community life and the apostolate. The non-residency programs (Associate) introduces candidates to Marist life through workshops and retreats, spiritual direction and visitation.

Candidates for the Priesthood normally finish college before entering the novitiate. Candidates for the Brotherhood either obtain a degree or develop skills in the professional or manual arts.

The novitiate program concentrates on personal and spiritual growth, providing the individual with a deeper understanding of Marist life.

Marists then study theology and gain practical pastoral experience before being ordained or taking final vows.

Maryknoll Missioners

"Proclaiming the Gospel to Peoples of Every Culture"

History/Charism

Maryknoll is the popular name for the Catholic Foreign Mission Society of America. Founded by two diocesan priests, James A. Walsh and Thomas F. Price, Maryknoll was approved by the American bishops in 1911 to involve American Catholics in the task of spreading Christ's name and message overseas. Thus, American men and women are engaged in fulfilling the command Christ gave to his whole Church of going to teach all nations His Good News.

Maryknoll is especially dedicated to the poor, the oppressed, and to those least affected by the Gospel message. Maryknoll Missioners strive to bring these men and women the Good News of Christ's love and brotherhood. They work to build a better world in which peace, justice and freedom will replace fear, poverty and oppression.

Maryknoll trains young Americans to be missioners...Priests, Brothers and Lay Apostles. Today there are over 1,000 Maryknoll Missioners working for God and man in 25 countries around the world...in Asia, Africa and Latin America.

Ministry/Service

The primary purpose of Maryknoll is to bring the message of Christ's love and peace to remote corners of the world...to help establish Christian communities...to nurture and train local leadership and clergy with the goal of turning the running of the active communities over to the people themselves...and then to move on to another area to repeat the Christianizing process.

Local conditions are studied carefully and, within that cultural framework, efforts are made to provide the information, initial material assistance, training and motivation that will enable the local people either to initiate self-help projects or to join together to act for peaceful social advancement and justice. This involves teaching, public health, youth work, social development, establishing the rights and dignity of workers, basic technology and other humanitarian skills.

Maryknoll Missioners take on this role with the knowledge that spiritual development is not possible when basic human needs are not met.

Information about Christian Mission is emphasized in Maryknoll's multi-faceted media operations targeted towards the American public.

Formation Program

The formation of a Maryknoll Missioner is that time when a man "molds" his life for his future in mission. It is a time of learning, but it is also a time when a man can examine and test his own motives and find out whether, indeed, he has a vocation to serve God through Maryknoll.

Priestly Formation—6 or 7 years:

One year with fellow candidates and the Maryknoll staff at our residence in Cambridge, Massachusetts.

Two years at the Maryknoll School of Theology at Maryknoll, New York.

Two or three years in Overseas Training Program...an intensive period of language study and supervised mission experience overseas.

Final year at Maryknoll in preparation for Oath and Ordination.

Brotherly Formation—5 or 6 years:

Initial four months at Brothers' House in Kitchawan, about four miles from Maryknoll, New York.

One year living in community and working in South Bronx.

Six months preparation for Overseas Training Program.

Two or three years in Overseas Training Program.

Final year at Maryknoll in preparation for Final Oath.

Lay Missioner Formation—4 months:

Living in community and studying at Maryknoll, New York, before signing three year contract and going on assignment overseas. Language study overseas.

Specific Information

While we continue to recognize that Maryknoll Missioners are a community united in our efforts to serve God by helping others, every opportunity is given to the individual to use his God-given abilities to the fullest.

There are several vocation weekend programs scheduled throughout the year at various Maryknoll Houses. In addition, Maryknoll sponsors three and four week summer opportunities to experience mission overseas.

The aim of the summer programs, especially, is to give sincerely motivated young men the opportunity to experience an actual mission situation so that they can make realistically informed decisions about a vocation within Maryknoll.

Montfort Missionaries

"In the Footsteps of the Poor Apostles"

History/Charism

This is the path of the Montfort Missionaries, the path of the apostle who brings the Word of God to the contemporary world. It is a path that leads out to those who are thirsting to hear a word from the Lord—to the poor, the struggling, the marginal. The path leads to people on the fringes and to places where the church community needs to be developed.

This path began in France three hundred years ago with a man who was a storyteller, a preacher, a wanderer, an artist, a contemplative—St. Louis de Montfort. Fascinated by the presence of God in human reality and, above all, in Jesus, Louis walked the roads of western France telling the story of the gospel and helping other people see that story in their lives. He helped to renew the church by calling people to live out their commitment to follow Jesus—like Mary, the model of discipleship.

Ministry/Service

Louis de Montfort's path continued in the community he began, a small group which he hoped would walk in the footsteps of the poor apostles bringing to people the story of the good news of Jesus. The Montfortian path spread throughout the world. In the United States the path is followed by a small group of people who seek to preach the Word through a variety of ministries—through retreats and spiritual renewal programs, in parishes, in hospitals, in third world missions; but above all these ministries are with the poor and with developing church communities.

The way leads on to the future, to new contexts for ministry but ultimately it leads on to Jesus who is with us on the road. As we tell the story of Jesus, we seek to renew ourselves and those with whom we minister, and we look for others who would be with us on the road.

We look for people who are alive in their commitment to follow Jesus.

We look for people who are committed to speak the Good News to the poor... people who want to listen to the story of Jesus as it is written in the Scriptures and in the world.

We look for people who, like Mary, want to listen to the Word, ponder the Word, and help to give the Word flesh today.

We look for people who are free to face the ambiguities of the road as together we renew our community and our church, as we bring a word of salvation to the people.

Formation Program

Montfort Affiliate Program: This is a program for people of college age and older who want to discover if they are called to a life of ministry. Affiliates meet regularly with a spiritual guide, and they meet periodically with other members of the program for retreats and workshops. They also have the opportunity to participate in summer ministry and community experiences.

A commitment to the affiliate program is not a commitment to enter the community. It is simply a commitment to search out your vocation in life.

Candidacy: Men interested in being a part of the Montfort Community can apply for candidacy after spending time in the affiliate program. The candidate lives in a community house and begins experiencing the ministry and life-style of the Montfort Missionaries. It is a time to learn more about the community and to discern with a spiritual guide whether this is their calling.

Novitiate: This is the first official step of entering the community, a way of beginning to walk the Montfortian path. It is a year of intense prayer, learning and reflection. Presently, our novitiate house is located in Washington, D.C.

Norbertines
Daylesford Abbey

"Building a Family of Faith-filled Friends"

History/Charism

"The whole group of believers was united, heart and soul; no one claimed for his own use anything that he had, as everything they owned was held in common. The apostles continued to testify to the resurrection of the Lord Jesus with great power..." (Acts 5:32-33).

This is the dream our Spiritual Father, Saint Augustine dreamed in the fourth century as the Bishop of Hippo. Through it he was able to help renew the Church in North Africa. This is the dream our Founder, Saint Norbert, dreamed in 1120 when he founded the Order of Premontre in a deserted valley in France. Through it he was able to help renew the Church in medieval Europe. This is the dream we continue to dream as contemporary Norbertines. Through it we hope to help renew God's Church in America. It is the same dream which animated the community of Christ's first apostles. When we find ourselves being true to this dream, we give God praise. When we find ourselves being unfaithful to it, we do penance.

Following the example of Christ's apostles and the Spirit of Saint Augustine, we try to live as brothers in faith and to strike a creative balance between a life of intense prayer and a life of selfless service to God's people. Central to our way of growing together spiritually are the meditative reading of God's Word, liturgical prayer in public, the prayerful celebration of the Eucharist and the daily give-and-take of our shared life and ministry. Our vows sum up this spirituality in terms of a life-long conversion to becoming more Christlike by living more simply, more chastely and more obediently. Our community includes both priests and brothers, although, in recent years, there have been few candidates for the brotherhood.

Ministry/Service

As Canons Regular of Premontre, we try to live, build, and celebrate authentic Christian community wherever we are. This basic mission has generated many different forms of ministry for us over the centuries, depending on the signs of the times and the needs of the local Church. At present, our ministerial focus in America is on preaching, teaching, liturgy, and various forms of pastoral activity.

Formation Program

The formal preparation for our life and ministry takes six or more years and unfolds in two main phases: the preparation for communal living and the preparation for communal ministry.

The first phase of our formation focuses on the *preparation for communal living*. It begins in an exploratory way, with entrance into our pre-novitiate program. It continues in an intense way, through a two-year novitiate experience and through a three-year experience of temporal profession in the community. This first phase of formation is completed when the candidate is fully incorporated into the life of the community through solemn vows. Up to this point, the preparation for brothers and priests in the community is identical.

The second phase of our formation focuses on the *preparation for communal ministry*. It begins with occasional experiences of volunteer work and of participation in the community's apostolates and continues in an intense way, in a four-year program of preparation for ministry at our House of Studies in Chicago. This second phase of formation is completed when the candidate is fully incorporated into the community's priestly ministry through ordination and his first ministerial assignment by the community.

Norbertine Fathers & Brothers
St. Norbert Abbey

"A Renewed Spirit"

History/Charism

The Norbertine Fathers & Brothers of St. Norbert Abbey have over 850 years of tradition behind them. The Abbey—the spiritual and community headquarters in this country—is part of an Order that is among the oldest in the Church. The Norbertines were founded in 1120 by Norbert of Xanten (Germany), the saint who was a contemporary of St. Bernard of Clairvaux and who is known as the Apostle of the Blessed Sacrament. Norbert founded his Order in the Premontre Valley of France (Diocese of Laon).

This accounts for the various names by which the Order is known: Norbertine after the Order's founder; Praemonstratensian after the place where the Order was founded; and Canons Regular of Premontre after the legal title given to those religious who say the office in common and live a community life.

Norbertines have been in South America since the 17th century. The first permanent foundation in the United States was made by Abbot Bernard H. Pennings, who came to Wisconsin in 1893 from Berne Abbey in Holland.

Norbertines are religious priests and brothers who follow the Rule of St. Augustine and take the three vows of poverty, celibacy, and common life.

Ministry/Service

An important dimension of our ministry and way of life is in prayer and in the common life we share in community. We also offer opportunities for ministry in teaching, in service to the poor, in pastoral ministry, in the missions in Lima, Peru, and in administration and management.

Formation Program

The Formation Program distinguishes three stages of initiation:

1. Affiliation is the process by which the aspirant is afforded a preliminary acquaintance with the life and work of the Norbertine Community under the guidance of a Norbertine. We accept candidates to the Order after two years of college.

2. Incorporation is initiation and gradual integration of a candidate into the life of a community; it begins with admission to Novitiate and concludes with perpetual profession.

3. Preparation for ministry presupposes affiliation and incorporation; it is a program with its own professional norms, finding its completion for the clerical candidate in Ordination to the Priesthood.

Specific Information

The Norbertine tradition and experience is one of shared life, shared prayer and shared ministry.

This experience is reinforced by our new *Mission Statement* developed in early 1984—and is as follows:

Christ and the Church call us, the members of St. Norbert Abbey, to be a community of one mind and heart on the way to God, in a manner consistent with the Gospel, the spirit of our founders and the constitutions of our Order.

We, therefore, dedicate ourselves to be bound together in communal relationship, strengthened by a commitment to life-long conversion, and service to the world. We embrace those persons already dedicated to our mission and welcome the association of other men and women with us.

God summons us to hear and proclaim the Good News of Salvation and the Kingdom of love, justice and mercy.

We commit ourselves to this ministry of the Word. We promise to witness the reality of Salvation and the Kingdom in our Common Life and to help make this message and experience available to all the people we serve.

Jesus the Lord, challenges us to adopt a spirituality, enriched by liturgical celebration, personal prayer and a journey of faith to the Kingdom.

We resolve to embrace a poverty that reflects a simplicity of life, a celibacy that opens us to growth in the Spirit in union with men and women, and obedience that makes us attentive to God's word. We dedicate ourselves to a life of self-giving rooted in the Eucharist and Common Prayer. This is the environment for our apostolic formation, reconciliation and our lifelong personal and spiritual growth.

The Spirit lays a claim on us to engage, within our capabilities, in a variety of ministries, to the People of God and the world at large.

We place ourselves at the service of people's needs, with special emphasis on service and advocacy for the poor. We commit ourselves to our traditional ministries, while being open to new apostolates. We strive to live with the tensions that are associated with the relationship between contemplation and action, community life and apostolates.

God urges us to face the future with openness, hope and courage.

We, the members of St. Norbert Abbey, inspired by Mary our Mother and Norbert our founder, move into our future with its diverse challenges in a spirit of faith and hope. In union with Christ, we wholeheartedly devote ourselves and our resources to further the Lord's work.

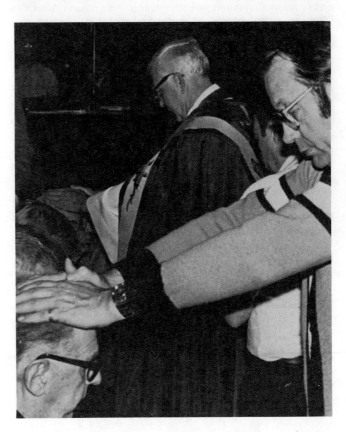

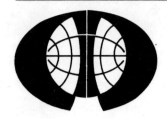

Missionary Oblates of Mary Immaculate

"Offering Themselves to the Service of God and His People"

History/Charism

"To preach the Gospel to the poor he has sent me." (Lk. 4:18) That vision of Jesus' mission inspired Blessed Eugene de Mazenod, founder of the Missionary Oblates of Mary Immaculate. It continues to inspire today's 6,000 Oblate priests and brothers. Those served by Blessed Eugene in the wake of the French Revolution are seen in today's neglected, poor, and abandoned, for riches, power and societal attitudes currently enslave millions of people, preventing the fullness and wholeness of life in the Spirit.

Oblates are literally "offered ones." They commit themselves to Christ, Church, and each other in community and mission as "specialists in the most difficult missions," in Pius XI's words. They strive to evangelize the poor out of their own poverty, taking Christ and each other seriously, hospitably, joyfully. In this line, the American region recently committed itself to the goals of a) ministry to minorities, especially Hispanics, b) development of lay ministries, c) Oblate reform and renewal, and d) concern for issues of justice and peace.

Ministry/Service

Oblates live and work in more than 40 countries in several thousand locations, with almost 1000 members in the five American provinces. The specific ministry for the individual results from discernment of personal talents and abilities, the needs of the local Church, and Oblate provincial commitments. Present ministries are greatly varied: urban, rural and suburban parishes; chaplaincies in hospitals, prisons and the armed services; native American missions, retreat houses, shrines, social ministries, foreign missions, and many others.

Formation Program

Oblate formation programs for potential brothers or priests serve high school, college or post-college age men. The high school seminaries, college residences near private colleges or universities, and associate programs prepare candidates for the Central U.S. novitiate in Godfrey, IL. Oblates from the several provinces staff this program as a team. A year's pre-novitiate is designed for degreed men who have not experienced Oblate college formation settings. As arranged by the governing province, theology students attend the Graduate Theological Union in Berkeley, Oblate School of Theology in San Antonio, the Boston Theological Union in Cambridge, Oblate College in Washington, or the International Scholasticate in Rome. Preparation for the Oblate brotherhood stresses full training according to personal abilities and talents.

Oblates of St. Francis de Sales

"There Is Nothing So Strong as Gentleness and Nothing So Gentle as Real Strength"

History/Charism

The above "gentleness-strength" quotation originated with—and was lived by—St. Francis de Sales.

Francis was born in France. He grew up to be a priest and bishop. As bishop, he co-founded the Sisters of the Visitation. His death in 1622 halted plans to establish a religious congregation of priests and brothers.

The Visitation Sisters never forgot Francis' plan.

Through the encouragement of the Visitandines, a young parish priest, Louis Brisson, gathered together a small group of men to live the life of Jesus Christ in the spirit of St. Francis de Sales.

Since the founding in 1875 the Oblates have spread in ten countries. In the 1980's a thousand Oblates are proclaiming the vision of Francis de Sales, the "gentleman saint."

Ministry/Service

The Oblate family includes Brothers, Priests, and those still in training. They work closely together in all their apostolates trying to promote peace and justice in today's world.

Oblates are involved in all kinds of ministry, and what is most important to them is bringing the spirit of St. Francis to whatever they do. Currently the American Provinces are involved in: Education (high school & college), parish, foreign mission, retreat center, summer camp, inner city, peace and justice, chaplaincy: campus, hospital, military, nursing home and prison.

Formation

Becoming an Oblate priest or brother is a very personal matter. Following the lead of Francis de Sales, our formation program attempts to be highly personal and individualized, treating every person as a unique creation. The Oblates accept candidates age 18 and older.

After getting to know the Oblates and when deemed ready, the candidate moves into a community. As Oblate life is experienced, a decision is made concerning entrance into the Oblate Novitiate.

The Novitiate is a full year of study, prayer and reflecting on one's personal call to follow the Lord as an Oblate of St. Francis de Sales.

Following the Novitiate, annual vowed membership begins until the time is right for a life commitment as an Oblate priest or brother.

During all the years of formation, an Oblate is involved in schooling and/or work according to his gifts and the ministries for which he is preparing. The Oblate who is a candidate for priesthood must complete graduate theological training for ordination. The Oblate brother is encouraged to develop along the lines of those skills, abilities and interests which he has and which meet the needs of the congregation.

Congregation of the Oratory

"Blending the Secular Life of Ministry with Community Ideals"

History/Charism

St. Philip Neri was the founder of the Oratory in Rome. This was a gathering together of laymen with some priests, Bishops and even Cardinals attending the daily Exercises of the Oratory. At these Exercises there was extemporary prayer, spontaneous teaching on the Word of God, inspired music (Oratorio), preaching by laymen, works of mercy and charity performed by the group. It became a leavening and reforming force of Rome. Priests and laymen gathered under St. Philip's direction to care for the rapidly growing lay movement. They began living communally and finally were formalized into a community under the title of Congregation of the Oratory in order to perpetuate and continue the Oratory. This was July 15, 1575.

The distinctive mark of this Congregation was that its members were priests and clerics who remained seculars and never became "Religious". Each house of the Congregation was independent from all others and there was no central power or administration. There is no profession of Evangelical Counsels as in religious orders nor transfer from house to house. One lives and dies in one's own Congregation doing the things that have to be done in that locale.

Its special charism or giftedness is prayer—"living in an atmosphere of prayer." It especially stands for service, freely given and volunteered. It has an intense community life, seeks to remain small. Its members retain their own money and goods, seeking only detachment, not renunciation. The Rock Hill Oratory was founded in South Carolina in 1934. Since then it has been doing exactly this.

Ministry/Service

The mission of the Rock Hill Oratory is:
- to search the Gospel and joyfully live the charisms of St. Philip Neri in a ministry of prayer, proclamation of the Word and social justice.
- to be challenged and affirmed in a community that is unique in its government, communal in its approach to ministry and a faithful steward of its alms;
- to be accepting of personal charisms, developing a shared ministry with the laity and actively promoting the renewal and service of the local church.

Formation Program

The Rock Hill Oratory has always integrated new members into the on-going life of our house. Our formation process is based on candidates meeting, sharing and living with our experienced members.

Formation means that new members share in our prayer and liturgical life; that they review and learn basic theology and spirituality; and especially that we share our charism, Constitutions and planning process.

We are responsible to introduce our candidates to the Catholic experience in the western Carolinas; into ecumenical activities in a state that is 2% Roman Catholic; and finally into the many parish and special ministries of our Community.

Pallottines

"Empowering the Laity to Roles of Leadership"

History/Charism

Our official title is The Society of the Catholic Apostolate (S.A.C.). The community was formed in 1835 by a true visionary, St. Vincent Pallotti. While Vincent was chronologically a 19th century priest, his concepts and ideas of the Church pushed him ahead into the 20th century, in the very heart of Vatican II.

The vision of St. Vincent was the Church in miniature. His concept was that of a community which embraced not only priests, brothers and sisters but most especially the laity. Such a view was unusual for his time. The great majority of founders of religious institutions centered their concern on the special mission of priests, brothers and sisters. Pallotti was interested in the spiritual formation of the laity and it was his deep desire to incorporate the laity into the Society of the Catholic Apostolate. His goal and purpose remain today the primary principle of the Pallottines. To be a Pallottine requires a full understanding and dedication to St. Vincent's vision and goals.

Pope Pius XII beatified Vincent Pallotti in 1950, and the beloved Pope John XXIII, during the Second Vatican Council, declared him a saint in 1963. Both pontiffs recognized that his vision was far into the future.

Ministry/Service

The Pallottines are engaged in apostolic works all over the world, touching every inhabitable continent. Our international community maintains the universal goal to spread the message of the Gospel in all languages to all people (Mt. 28:19-20). Our inspiration comes from that great moment of Pentecost, when the Holy Spirit gave the Apostles the power to speak in many tongues so that everyone would understand.

The goal of the Pallottines in the United States is to present this universal vision of charity and Christ's message to our fellow citizens. Often the tasks are mundane yet very demanding. Each priest and brother is asked to serve and to educate the people he meets. Our primary task then is to form, to maintain, and to enrich a community of believers.

In the United States our work is primarily pastoral. It takes many forms; but whether it be presiding over liturgical celebrations, counseling in marriage, visiting the sick, helping the needy, conducting adult education or facilitating youth formation programs, it is with the vision of forming a true Christian community and empowering all to use their gifts for the service of the gospel— the crux of our call.

There is no room for the egocentric person in the Pallottine community. There is simply the need for complete charity, mutual participation, and acceptance of co-responsibility for the goal that was set by Jesus Christ. This was the vision of Pallotti and continues to be the cornerstone of the Pallottine community.

Formation Program

We welcome dedicated individuals of any age to the community. Formal entrance, however, would be initiated after a time of discernment with the vocation director and the completion of all high school requirements. Once accepted, the candidate begins a pre-profession period of at least two years. The first year (postulancy) enables the candidate to experience community life, further his formal education and begin to set a good spiritual foundation. Following this year, the candidate then moves to St. Louis (an inter-Novitiate program of both Provinces and Canada) for a year of intense prayer, study and reflection. The candidate then begins his temporary profession period, which lasts a minimum of three to a maximum of six years in which he continues his education either for the Priesthood or the Brotherhood.

Specific Information

There are two Provinces in the United States. The Mid-West Province based in Milwaukee, Wisconsin and the Eastern Province, based in Pennsauken, New Jersey. Our apostolates too are universal including parishes, education, hospital and retreat work, in a word, any activity that fosters the spreading of faith and the increase of charity.

Servants of the Paraclete

"To Support Fellow Workers in Ministry"

History/Charism

In Father Gerald Fitzgerald's early life as a diocesan priest, then as a Holy Cross Religious, and later as an army chaplain during World War II, he became increasingly aware of the particular needs of his fellow priests who were experiencing conflicts and difficulties. Because of this developing consciousness he experienced an unfolding vision. As time went on, he realized more clearly the need to have a Congregation of religious to sustain and amplify this vision. The Servants of the Paraclete, a young Congregation of priests and brothers dedicated to help and support their fellow workers in the ministry, was founded in 1947 in Jemez Springs, New Mexico by Father Gerald.

Ministry/Service

Today, as they continue to expand upon the vision of Father Gerald, the Servants of the Paraclete operate various programs.

There are three programs in Jemez Springs, NM: Foundation House, a renewal center for priests and brothers suffering from stress and emotional difficulties; Villa Louis Martin, a center for the treatment of psychological and psychiatric difficulties; Our Lady of Lourdes, a retirement center.

In St. Louis, MO, there is St. Michael's Center for the Holistic Treatment of Chemical Dependency. There are halfway houses in Canton, OH, and Cherry Valley, CA. In Brownshill, England there is a center for the treatment of chemical dependency and emotional difficulties. Programs are in the planning stages in Rome and Montopali, Italy.

The Congregation numbers some 50 priests, brothers and clerics who bring hope and health to their fellow ministers.

The Servants of the Paraclete have a variety of training and background. Their professional competence includes training in Theology, Scripture and Ministry, nursing, psychology, psychotherapy, psychiatry, alcoholism counseling, clinical pastoral education, spiritual direction and pastoral experience. They also employ a number of lay people who function in these roles to help them in their ministry.

The Servants of the Paraclete approach is holistic. They live as a family with strong ties to prayer, interaction and service. They invite their brothers to join this family in order to share in the warmth and goodness of God's presence. This family life can help a man tear away the roles of priest or brother so that he can see himself as an individual human being. It gives him access to his physical, emotional, spiritual, intellectual, and psychological strengths and weaknesses, enabling him to deal with himself as a total person.

Whatever the particular reason for visiting one of the Servants of the Paraclete houses, each brother and priest experiences a brother-to-brother relationship while there. They are warmly welcomed, encouraged to be at home and to make use of all facilities, to share community, to talk about their ideas, hopes, fears, conflicts, or plans in an atmosphere of congeniality and peace.

Formation Program

A person interested in joining the Congregation is asked to live as an Associate in one of the houses of the Servants of the Paraclete for a minimum of 9 months. After this assessment period, the Associate will enter the Novitiate. Incorporation into the Religious Life begins with the Novitiate. These two years are spent in acquainting oneself with the lifestyle of the members, prayer, study of the Constitutions, and apostolic work. At the end of the Novitiate a person makes first profession of the vows of poverty, chastity and obedience. The Novitiate can be followed by educational pursuits. Candidates for the priesthood will finish their theological training at a university or seminary and then go on to specialize in some area related to the ministry (e.g. counseling). A brother can begin this specialized training at the end of the Novitiate period. All educational training is in keeping with the specific apostolate of the Congregation. After three years of temporary vows a member is eligible for perpetual profession. Formation does not stop with the end of this period. The Servants of the Paraclete believe that formation continues until death and help one another in the process of life.

Specific Information

As a community of men in service to their fellow brothers and priests, the apostolate of the Servants of the Paraclete is open to meet the needs of the church in the modern world. The Servants of the Paraclete continue to reach out to help their fellow ministers on new levels and in new ways. And so, the Servants of the Paraclete today need new ministers as they ready themselves for contemporary commitments.

The Passionists

"Spirituality Centered on the Cross"

History/Charism

Each Passionist, whether brother or priest, is called to share his gifts with the Church. The gift or charism of the Community is to help bring meaning to the suffering in the lives of people. This permeates all our ministries.

Jesus' death on the cross was a death in the cause of justice. He was executed because he challenged accepted values. He sided with the poor and the outcasts. He condemned oppressive structures. Jesus was a prophet and prophets meet strong opposition.

His cross reminds us that Christians must listen to the cries of the poor. We are in solidarity with those whom society may forget or even exploit. The cross is a sign of justice. To remind the world about the cross is to challenge the world for its injustice and neglect. Through our founder, Paul Daneo, Passionists began responding to that challenge back in Italy in 1741. The challenge was carried to the United States where Passionists first came to Pittsburgh in 1852. Passionists are pledged to that challenge today, ministering from Boston to Los Angeles.

Ministry/Service

A ministry that was started by our founder, St. Paul of the Cross, is that of going into a parish for a few days or a week to renew the parish through the spoken word. This band of men moves around much like the early apostles. The Word is also shared through the production of radio and television programs, and by our presence in hospitals, classrooms, campuses, missions and those ministries of service to the community.

Ministering to laity, religious and priests through our retreat centers is a vital part of our activity. Providing special programs for couples, alcoholics, young singles, youth, senior citizens, etc., keeps our centers busy.

Ministry within the Passionist Community has always been valued as an integral part of our total ministry to the Church. Whether one is involved in making a community a comfortable place to live, in administration, or preparing food for the table, all are important.

Ministry as a Passionist brother in the Church and Community offers a wide diversity of opportunities. Teachers, cooks, administrators, carpenters, accountants, parochial ministers, nurses—all fit well into a brother's call. Through working in our community apostolates or on the job with the laity, the brother shares a powerful witness of the religious lifestyle.

Passionist Missionaries are working in the Philippines, Japan, Korea, India and the West Indies helping the local Church to develop.

Formation Program

Entering the Passionist community is a process that involves you in the life of Passionists, in the life of the whole Church and in the life of the world that both serve.

Associate Program—Generally six months to one year of vocational counseling and spiritual direction.

Residence or Pre-Novitiate Program—A one to two year period of living in a Passionist Community completing one's education and/or taking part in the work and life of the community.

Novitiate—A one year program of studying Christian and Passionist life. Through prayer and spiritual direction one makes his first commitment or declaration of "at homeness" in the Passionist Community.

Post-Novitiate—Those called to the prietshood take four years of theological studies. Those called to brotherhood pursue further professional and theological training to carry on their ministries. For personal growth and as ministers in the contemporary Church, all Passionists are engaged in ongoing formation and continuing education.

The Society of St. Paul

"Using the Mass Media of Communications to Spread the Ever-New Message of Christ"

History/Charism

United in the idea that the modern techniques of communications should be used to spread the Catholic message of salvation to modern men and women, the Society of St. Paul has grown in little over sixty years from a small group of dedicated men into a congregation of priests and brothers with communities in 23 countries.

At the time the Society was founded, only a visionary could foresee a world-wide network of brothers and priests employing the communications media to accomplish God's work on earth while living an authentic religious life. But even this visionary, the priest who founded the Society of St. Paul in 1914, Father James Alberione, could not imagine in those early days what tremendous advances would be made in the field of communications during the coming years—automatic typesetting equipment was just invented; motion pictures were still a novelty, and television was not even in the dictionary.

We may marvel that a ministry of communications could have been started in such an early part of our century, but started it was, and what's more it has matured and flourished in the intervening years.

sage of God's love far and wide. In conjunction with a life of prayer, contemplation, study and community, Paulines are editors, writers, technicians, photographers, graphic artists, proofreaders, printers, sound engineers, mechanics, advertising and bookstore managers—in short, according to individual talents and needs of the community, they may act in any phase of the Society's developing communications ministry.

To reach the greatest number of people, to touch their lives by using the far-reaching means of communications—this is the core mission of the Society of St. Paul—following in the footsteps of their model St. Paul and their founder Father James Alberione.

Formation Program

The candidate for the Priesthood or Brotherhood enters the Society of St. Paul at Canfield, Ohio (near Youngstown) for his postulancy (first year) where he starts to become familiar with Pauline life and ministry. After this, he begins a one year Novitiate in which he studies the constitutions, the vows of poverty, chastity, obedience and fidelity to the Pope. At the completion of Novitiate he makes his first profession of temporary vows. He then begins his scholastic studies at the Society of St. Paul Community on Staten

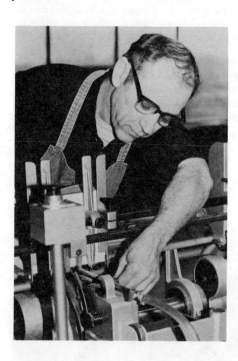

Until his death in 1971, Father Alberione continued to direct and inspire the many activities of his young community. He also founded the Daughters of St. Paul, the Sister Disciples of the Divine Master, the Pastoral Sisters and the Queen of Apostles Sisters and four secular institutes. His spiritual sons and daughters, known as the Pauline Family, number over 7000 members.

Ministry/Service

The Pauline Priests and Brothers are engaged in a challenging ministry, producing religious and inspirational books, cassettes, films, filmstrips, records, bibles and broadcasts to spread the mes-

Island, New York. Depending on his talents and prior college courses (if any), these range from undergraduate to graduate studies so that he will be ready for the demands of the communications apostolate. The facilities of nearby colleges, universities and seminaries are utilized.

Specific Information

Worldwide, the Society of St. Paul operates radio and television stations, book and media centers, recording and film production facilities and over twenty publishing houses producing a variety of books, bibles, magazines and other Catholic literature.

Paulists

"Our American character is suitable for a certain type of spiritual perfection. An attempt to bring out any other or impose any other on it will be unsuccessful, if not fatal, in many instances... So far as it is compatible with faith and piety, I am for accepting the American civilization with its usage and custom; leaving aside other reasons, it is the only way by which Catholicity can become the religion of our people. The character and spirit of our people and their institutions, must find themselves at home in our church in a way those of other nations have done; and it is on that basis alone that the Catholic religion can make progress in our country."
Isaac Hecker,
Founder of the Paulists

Isaac Hecker had a vision for the church in America. When he founded the Paulists in 1858, Father Hecker had a vision of a dynamic and growing Church. He sought dynamic men with personal initiative fueled by the Holy Spirit to help turn his vision into reality. As the first order of priests founded in the United States, their original mission was to convert the unchurched in America to the Catholic faith. This goal broadened as their numbers grew and the church grew and changed, for the Paulists were determined to grow and change with it. Striking a balance between personal freedom and commitment to the teaching of the church, an atmosphere was created that nurtured creativity and innovation which allowed them to retain their personal individuality and to adapt to and facilitate growth and change in social conditions.

Ministry/Service

Today the Paulists are recognized as an innovative and effective force throughout the United States and Canada. Though numbering only 250 members, the community continues to spread God's word on an individual and public level. They work with the poor and underprivileged. They work in ecumenism and in downtown information centers and campus ministries. Through their work in the media, operating Paulist Press, the largest U.S. distributor of Catholic literature and doing television and film work including the Emmy award-winning "Insight" series, the Paulists continue to reach thousands, with a style that is uniquely Paulist.

Formation

Paulist formation begins with a novitiate program lasting one year, which is open to college graduates. This introduction to community combines prayer and apostolic work with the ideas of personal freedom and responsibility which are central to Paulist philosophy. The novitiate ends with the making of first promises. These temporary promises are renewed at the end of the second and third year.

Immediately following novitiate, candidates move on to at least three years at St. Paul's College in Washington, D.C. where they complete graduate studies in theology at Catholic University or The Washington Theological Union. After completing theology and apostolic training, the Paulist is ordained a deacon and serves one year internship at a Paulist foundation. Ordination to the priesthood comes at the end of that year.

The Piarists

"Dedicated to Education of the Young"

History/Charism

Our religious order, the Order of the Pious Schools or the Piarists, was officially established by Pope Gregory XV on November 18, 1621. At that time our Founder and first Superior General, St. Joseph Calasanz was sixty-two years old, and he had already been laboring since April 9, 1597 to found a religious community which would be dedicated to the Christian education of children, particularly the poor.

He wanted a religious order of men with solemn vows and not subject to any ordinaries except the Bishop of Rome. As religious and teachers, they would dedicate themselves not only to the teaching of reading, writing, arithmetic, but also Latin, other languages and grammar; this formal dedication is assured by our fourth solemn vow of special concern for the education of children. As priests, they would also dedicate themselves to the religious instruction and formation of youth and not to any other ministries common to other religious.

Ministry/Service

We teach on the elementary, secondary and university levels of academic education, and we minister to youth groups, for exam-

ple, the Boy Scouts, Catholic Youth Organizations and the like. We have our own schools on the elementary and secondary levels, and we cooperate with educators and parents in conducting and staffing a diocesan high school. Piarists also assist the clergy, religious and laity of local parishes through sacramental ministries.

Formation Program

a) *Pre-Novitiate:* One year residence at and cooperation in one of our communities and its school (omitted at the discretion of the Provincial).
b) *Novitiate:* One year of initiation into our lifestyle with its particular spirituality and personality.
c) *Juniorate:* Depending on one's college status, four to eight years of university studies: a B.A. or B.S. in one's area of teaching expertise and an M.A. in Sacred Theology; after B.A. or B.S., one year of practice teaching before theological studies.

Specific Information

The uniqueness of our community rests upon our fourth solemn vow. This vow gives a special direction to our life and its interpretation of Jesus Christ's command, "Go forth and teach all nations."

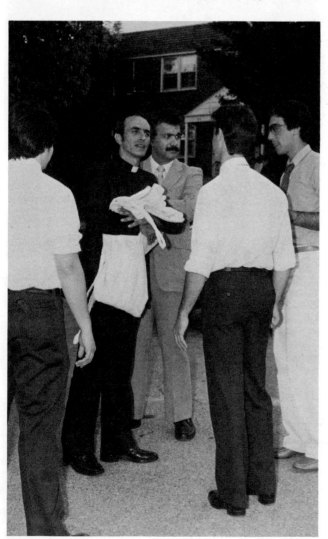

Society of the Precious Blood

"Making People Aware of the Mystery of Redemption"

History/Charism

The Society of the Precious Blood is an apostolic community of priests and brothers living the celibate, common life in the bond of charity and dedicated in a special way to the devotion of the Precious Blood.

Founded in 1815 by St. Gaspar del Bufalo, a priest of the Diocese of Rome, the Society quickly spread into Germany and the United States. It is in the United States that the Society had its greatest growth. From here, it established its work in South America, especially in Chile and Peru. In 1965, the single province of the Society in America was divided into three. The Province of the Pacific covers nine western states although the members are engaged in their apostolic activities primarily in the state of California. The Kansas City Province covers seventeen states in the Midwest with the members engaged in various apostolic activities in twelve of those states. The Cincinnati Province covers everything east of the Mississippi River and the members are engaged in varied apostolic ministries in nine of those states with missionaries in Chile and Peru.

Ministry/Service

The main task of the members of the Society of the Precious Blood is to serve the people of God. The Society has always prided itself on its ability to adapt and respond to special invitations from the bishops for any project which is especially needed in the Church. Precious Blood priests and brothers are engaged in retreat work, in prison, hospital, and military chaplaincies, in foreign missions, in college, in parishes, adult religious education, Newman chaplaincies and high school teaching. Through these apostolic works and the witness of their lives, they try to make people aware of the mystery of redemption as symbolized by Christ's Precious Blood.

Formation Program

Young men who wish to study for the priesthood or brotherhood may enter anytime after high school. The Society of the Precious Blood has designated certain schools and colleges which best aid the prospective candidate in understanding the spirit of the Community and discerning the will of God in their lives. Each Province also has non-residency programs for those who are seeking a life of priesthood and brotherhood but remain at home to finish school or to complete a personal task before joining a formation program.

Specific Information

Although members of the Society of the Precious Blood do not take the traditional vows, they are bound together by a promise of fidelity to the Society and its Constitutions and by a bond of fraternal charity. Therefore, no distinction is made between priest and brother except in the exercise of apostolic ministry. Each Precious Blood member knows that, even after the most challenging and tiresome day, he will be refreshed by the good natured give and take among the fellow members of the community house. This Community Spirit, this sense of belonging, is a real, constant experience for the members.

The Redemptorists

"Preachers of the Good News"

History/Charism

"They hardly even know the name of Jesus," the young priest exclaimed. He could hardly believe that, a few miles outside of the priest-rich city of Naples, shepherds and the rural poor knew practically nothing about the faith into which they were born. He had come into the countryside for a vacation and was to leave it with a new vision.

The young priest became St. Alphonsus Liguori, Doctor of the Church. In 1732 he gathered a small band of men around him to preach the Good News to "the poor and most abandoned." From this original group the Redemptorists developed and today are preaching the Good News in 57 countries on every continent of the globe.

The modern expression of the Redemptorist rule of life retains Alphonsus' vision and purpose. "The purpose of the Redemptorist Community is to follow the example of Jesus Christ, the Redeemer, by preaching the word of God to the poor, as He declared of Himself: 'He sent me to preach the Good News to the poor.' "

Redemptorists today are found in every form of apostolate because their work is not defined by law but by the spirit of their rule of life which urges them to "diligently seek out those people who are more deprived of spiritual help, especially the poor and the underprivileged." Addressing itself to the chaotic world of the 1980's, the rule of life recommends that Redemptorists work for "migrants, exiles, refugees, those who live and work in overcrowded areas of cities, and those who, because of race or color, see themselves unjustly excluded from the principal civil rights enjoyed by others."

Ministry/Service

Redemptorists in the United States staff parishes, operate retreat centers, engage in inner-city ministry, preach parish renewals, spread the Good News through publishing magazines, books, pamphlets, and other printed aids for parish service. They also concentrate on ministry to the deaf and to Hispanic minorities and have begun a new emphasis on the ministry to social justice. Redemptorists of the United States are also involved in missionary activity in Brazil, Thailand, Puerto Rico, the Virgin Islands, the Dominican Republic, and Paraguay.

Formation Program

Redemptorists operate two high school seminary programs, two college seminaries, a college center program (a college residence close to a major university), a theological seminary, a formation house of theology students and a common novitiate. A man interested in Redemptorist life as a brother or priest may enter at any level of the formation program, but is expected to spend at least one year in one of these Redemptorist communities before entering the one year novitiate.

Specific Information

It is difficult to describe what it is that makes Redemptorist life unique. Those who live it know that it is unique, know that they are called. It can, perhaps, be summed up in the flavor of community life which is interwoven with apostolic mission. As they seek to answer "the urgent pastoral needs of the church" in the various situations in which they find themselves, Redemptorists live together, work together, pray together, and try to be a team and a family. The rule of life sums it up:

Redemptorists are called to prolong in the world the presence of Christ and his mission of Redemption. They choose the Person of Christ as the center of their life, and they strive to become attached to him more intimately in personal union as each day goes by. Thus at the heart of the community to mold it and sustain it is Christ Himself, the Redeemer, and His Spirit of Charity.

The Resurrectionists

"A Loving, Supportive, Caring Brotherhood"

History/Charism

The Congregation of the Resurrection is a community of priests, deacons and brothers in the United States as well as in nine other countries. The Resurrectionist call is to live the Gospel message of Jesus as a loving, supportive, caring brotherhood—a faith community. The community strives zealously to overcome sin, ignorance, injustice, and misery which is so prevalent in our society today. Our work for men helps them to experience the hope, peace, joy and healing which the Risen Christ desires to share with them through various apostolic works and missionary endeavors.

Our community had its beginnings in Paris, France in 1836 under the leadership of a layman, Bogdan Janski. After Janski's early death in 1840, his two principal associates, Peter Semenenko and Jerome Kajsiewicz, continued to promote his ideas and live in community. The first common rule of life was written during the Lenten season of 1842 and became the basis for community life and personal growth in the Lord. And since the day of the first profession of vows fell on Easter Sunday, they were inspired to dedicate themselves to the Risen Savior and to call themselves the "Brothers of the Resurrection." The brothers saw themselves called to die to sin and to live with the Risen Christ in a new life devoted to the pursuit of truth and love in the education of youth and in pastoral ministry.

We are a small community of about 450 members worldwide. Our smallness in size is in itself a unique gift which allows us to develop our fellowship with one another in the Risen Lord as a family. As a community we are called to bring about our own personal resurrection by dying to our selfishness through our vows that Christ may dwell in us and act through us in bringing about the resurrection of our society. We feel a special call to stress our brotherly love for one another in community to help us remain faithful to our call and to challenge all persons whom we encounter to love one another. "Love each other as brothers should, and have profound respect for each other." (Rm 12:10)

Ministry/Service

The American Resurrectionist community is involved in various apostolates such as chaplaincies, retreat work, mission work, hospital ministry, clinics and individualized ministries. However, the main thrust of our Resurrection ministry is directed toward parish ministry and the education of youth. In the United States we staff high schools, parishes, a retreat house, missions, as well as work in specialized ministries. At the present time we serve the needs of the Church in Illinois, Missouri, Kentucky, Alabama, Florida, California, and Nevada. As the needs of the Church change, so will the places we serve.

Formation Program

Men of any age after high school who feel a call to grow in the Lord in community and to serve the Church are invited to search out that call in one of the community's formation programs:

Associate Program—This program is for young men, seniors in high school and older, who are interested in the community. It enables them to live at home while they investigate our Resurrection lifestyle and their own call from God in either their college or work situation. The program involves spiritual direction as well as two retreats with the community each year.

College-Seminary Formation—The individual lives in the seminary community house in St. Louis and learns more about our lifestyle by living it with us and attending school.

Novitiate—This is an entire year devoted to the serious task of prayer, reflection and the discernment of God's will with the guidance of the Director of Novices. It gives the individual the opportunity to have a closer look at the vows as well as our community life as Resurrectionists.

Post-Novitiate Formation—The individual pursuing priesthood or diaconate in the community enrolls in a program of theological studies at Resurrection Seminary in St. Louis as well as involving himself in supervised ministries. The individual pursuing brotherhood in the community either continues his studies at the Seminary in St. Louis or lives in a local community house and is involved in supervised ministry.

Brothers of the Sacred Heart

"To Develop Christian Attitudes and Commitment in the Young"

History/Charism

In 1821, following the French Revolution, Father André Coindre, a dynamic and zealous French priest, saw illiterate French youth—troubled, without values or faith—ganging up to vandalize towns. He recruited a small group of caring, dedicated religious men to reach out to these young people with a positive, helpful response to their cry for help. The Brothers these French youth found were the Brothers of the Sacred Heart. And for over 150 years, thousands of other men have followed in the footsteps of these first Brothers, united in the belief that they, too, have been called and sent to show the remarkable brotherhood God offers to men. Brothers of the Sacred Heart continue to bring André Coindre's response to young people all over the world, striving to build hope through caring, discipline, understanding, education, counsel and faith. The goal of the Brothers of the Sacred Heart is to bring Christ's love to others, especially the young. They are men who believe first of all that God is a loving Father. They wish to live this love and to help young people to realize it. They consecrate their whole lives to this goal, taking strength from meeting the Lord in prayer.

Ministry/Service

The Brothers of the Sacred Heart believe in education: a broad professional education for themselves so they can serve as teachers, counsellors, social workers, parish leaders, or any service role where Christian leadership is needed; and education for the young so they can grow in personal strength, right values, and deeper faith. Through their primary ministry of teaching and through all other forms of service, the Brothers strive to build up a strong people of God.

Formation Program

The *Associate Program* is designed for those young men who have expressed serious interest in the Brothers of the Sacred Heart and who are seeking assistance in making a decision about their future vocation. The purpose of the program is to acquaint the interested candidate with the apostolic, community and prayer life of the Brothers by involving the young man on a regular basis with the life and work of the Brothers. The *Pre-Novitiate* is a period of one or two years during which time the candidate actually lives with a community of Brothers and with other pre-novices, either completing his college degree work, or in some form of the apostolate if he already possesses his degree. Following a three-semester *Novitiate,* which includes an in-depth study of religious life and a deepening of one's personal life of faith and prayer, the candidate makes his first commitment for a period of one year as a Brother of the Sacred Heart.

Specific Information

Candidates are accepted after high school, during and after college. The main thrust of the Brothers is to develop Christian attitudes and commitment in the young whom they teach. A Brother dedicates himself to this purpose through his commitment to God by the vows of poverty, chastity, and obedience.

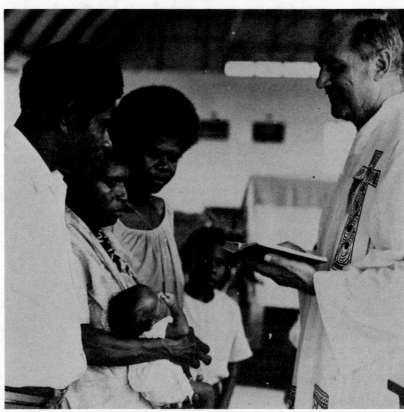

Missionaries of the Sacred Heart

"Accepting God's Love To Share with People in Need"

History/Charism

Missionaries of the Sacred Heart are called to make God's love known in their lives, especially through the words and deeds of evangelization. Founded in France in 1854, the society is now an international group of religious brothers and priests made up of 16 provinces around the globe with a total membership of about 2500. More than 950 members are at work in Latin America, Africa, Asia and Oceania.

What the Missionaries of the Sacred Heart are really all about can be seen in the words of their founder, Father Jules Chevalier: "Man's greatest need, if he is to find meaning and happiness, is to learn to believe in God's love for him and to let that love transform his life." All else is insignificant in comparison to an experience of the Father's love. Only in that love can a person surely and truly say: I am.

Taken by this truth, Missionaries of the Sacred Heart wish to share it with others. On this account they look to the kindness and compassion of the Heart of Christ as an essential charism, and they follow the tradition of an apostolic spirituality wherein the worth of any service depends on the measure of God's love that it reveals to others.

Ministry/Service

Consistent with their belief in the incomparable value of God's love, Missionaries of the Sacred Heart accept as a first concern the evangelization of people who have never heard the Good News of God's mercy and love. The United States Province acknowledges a special commitment to the young church in Papua, New Guinea and to the resurgent church in Colombia, Latin America.

Within the United States, the members feel called to mediate a deeper sense of God's love to His people by serving as preachers and spiritual directors, in pastoral ministry and as specialists in other Church-related services.

Formation Program

Working through a formation board, the Missionaries of the Sacred Heart maintain a readiness to accept candidates with differing educational experience and training needs. Ordinarily, candidates who enter on the college level complete this part of their education at the MSC College Residence at Allentown College, Center Valley, Pennsylvania. Applicants who have already completed their college studies join the community at Center Valley to have an opportunity to experience religious life and to take any supplementary courses that may be required in philosophy or theology before going on to Novitiate which is conducted at Youngstown, Ohio.

Brother and priest candidates continue their studies and formation at Catholic Theological Union in Chicago, Illinois, where a four-year program in theology and practical learning for ministry is available along with training in specialized trades and fields at other schools in the area.

Specific Information

Missionaries of the Sacred Heart welcome interested candidates to visit with MSC communities. Information on where major communities are located can be secured from the vocation director. The society motto is: "May the Sacred Heart of Jesus be loved everywhere."

Congregation of the Sacred Hearts

"Aspiring to the Spirit of Love of a Father Damien"

History/Charism

In the climate of fear and persecution of the French Revolution a young man, who had been ordained secretly in March, 1792, left the cramped attic where he had been hiding, knelt under an oak tree and offered his life to God. His name was Peter Coudrin. At great danger to his life, he spent the next several years ministering in disguise to the people in and around the city of Poitiers.

He waited for an opportune moment to found a religious congregation, for he had become aware during his forced hiding in the granary that God was calling him to do this. In 1794, he met Henriette Aymer de la Chevalerie, who had also undergone a profound religious experience while imprisoned by the revolutionaries for hiding a priest. On Christmas Eve, 1800, they founded a community of men and women dedicated to spreading the good news of God's unconditional love through devotion to the Sacred Hearts of Jesus and Mary and atoning for the sins of humanity through perpetual adoration of the Blessed Sacrament.

The members of the community were soon engaged in a variety of apostolates: schools, especially for the poor; the direction of diocesan seminaries; parish missions, and in 1827, were the first Catholic missionaries to go to the islands of the Pacific. When the founder died in 1837, the Community numbered 276 brothers and 1125 sisters.

Ministry/Service

Today the Sacred Hearts Community is established in some forty countries and has missions in the Pacific, Asia, Africa, South America and even in Europe—in Norway. The United States has three Provinces: the East Coast, the West Coast and the Hawaiian Provinces.

The East Coast Province has its main mission in Japan and also has missionaries in the Bahamas, Ecuador, and India, where two of its members have the spiritual care of leprosaria run by the Mis-

sionaries of Charity. Home missions, parish and inner city ministry, retreat work, chaplaincies and the Enthronement of the Sacred Heart in the Home are also works of the Province.

The West Coast Province works in four high schools, three parishes, seven chaplaincies, retreat work, Charismatic Renewal, TV Ministry, and operates a Novitiate for all four English Speaking Provinces.

Formation Program

In the East Coast Province, candidates for the priesthood are accepted after they have completed two years of college. Following a three month pre-novitiate program and a one year novitiate, candidates make a temporary profession of the evangelical counsels. After profession candidates who have completed four years of college begin their theological studies at the Washington Theological Union. Candidates for the brotherhood are accepted after completing two years of further education or work experience after high school. A postulancy of at least six months is required before going on to novitiate. Following temporary profession, at the end of the novitiate year, candidates for the brotherhood continue their spiritual and technical studies in preparation for apostolic involvement.

In the West Coast Province, candidates for priesthood are accepted after college; for brotherhood after having completed at least one year of work after high school. A pre-novitiate is required followed by a one year Novitiate. Candidates for priesthood begin their Theological studies at the Graduate Theological Union of Berkeley.

Specific Information

Community is a vital part of the Congregation's life and the "family spirit" one of its most treasured values. Community and apostolic life is enriched by the fact that the Congregation is a family with two branches, men and women. The life of the Community has a particular accent: the contemplation of the person of Jesus who is the sign of God's love for all people, and of the Mother of the Lord who is the model of belief in love. This love inspired the work of Father Damien for the lepers of Molokai.

The Eucharistic celebration is the center of daily life and throughout the life of the Congregation, adoration before the Blessed Sacrament has had a special importance in the formation and life of the Community.

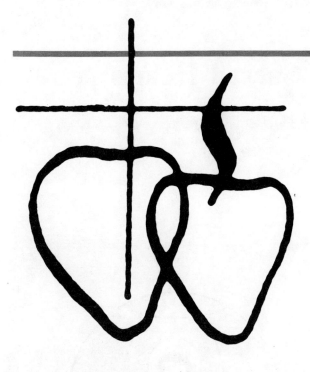

Missionaries of the Sacred Hearts of Jesus and Mary

"Dedicated to Making People Aware of God's Love for Them"

History/Charism

Naples, Italy, in the first part of the nineteenth century was ravaged by the Jansenist heresy which put fear above love, and kept many Christians away from God's Word and Sacraments. A diocesan priest, Cajetan Errico, was so deeply distressed by the situation that he gathered a group of priests about him, prayed with them for the Lord's guidance, and in October, 1833, began the work of the Missionaries of the Sacred Hearts. The new community immediately took to the streets, the pulpit and the homes of the people. They were, in the words of the constitutions of the congregation, "dedicated in works, studies, hardships, and life itself, to spreading among the people the very ardent love which the Sacred Hearts have for them, and in enkindling in them the fire of Divine Love."

The Congregation was approved by Pope Pius IX in September, 1846, and the fathers and brothers increased in number throughout the South of Italy, carrying out mission work which the people responded to very warmly. Yet after the suppression laws of 1861, the brothers of Cajetan Errico found themselves dispersed in various parts, seemingly lost in the confusion of the era. But the work of the Sacred Hearts did not die, for neither the Congregation nor the people would let it, and slowly the missionary apostolate regained strength, moving forward to meet the needs of this century.

Ministry/Service

From the beginning of the community until today, the primary work of the community has been to spread devotion to the Sacred Hearts of Jesus and Mary. This is accomplished through a variety of ministries. The priests and brothers strive to promote the social reign of the Sacred Heart through the Immaculate Heart of Mary by ministering in parishes, home and foreign missions and preaching. We seek to strengthen the family as the domestic church through the Enthronement of the Sacred Heart in the Home and the Pilgrim Virgin of Fatima Apostolate. Presently, the community undertakes these works in the Eastern United States, Italy, Argentina and Uruguay. Plans are being laid for a mission soon to be opened in India.

Formation Program

We accept candidates for both the priesthood and brotherhood. There is an affiliate program open to high school graduates with options for residency or non-residency. The residents attend Holy Apostles College in Cromwell, Connecticut. Novitiate occurs somewhere between the completion of second year college and graduation. The novitiate takes place in Linwood, New Jersey.

Theology is generally taken at Holy Apostles College in Cromwell. Special attention is given to delayed vocations. Candidates for the brotherhood should have completed high school and have several years of work experience or a skill. After novitiate, they will either seek training in some area or be assigned to one of the apostolates of the community.

Specific Information

Our Congregation is a small community of priests and brothers which lives a close family style of life. Our life together is based on the shared value we place on promoting devotion to the Sacred Hearts of Jesus and Mary. This shared goal gives life and meaning to all our apostolates. Through our own family life together, we hope to learn the values which we must present to the families to which we minister as we try to help them become the domestic churches they are called to become. In a word, our aim is the transformation of the Christian family.

Salesians of Don Bosco

"Signs and Bearers of God's Love for the Young"

History/Charism

St. John Bosco began working with young people shortly after his ordination in 1841 when his native Italy was entering the industrial age. The plight of many homeless and exploited boys moved him with fatherly concern to work on their behalf.

The handful of teenagers that met for Mass, religious instruction and recreation soon grew into the hundreds. As his mission took shape, Don Bosco invited 18 of these young men to join him in forming a religious community and dedicate themselves to young people. They called themselves the Society of St. Francis de Sales, the Salesians.

Don Bosco's heart went out to all young people. What began as a simple religion lesson and games in a narrow alley grew to a world-wide ministry to youth.

Ministry/Service

Salesians are not just youth ministers. Like Don Bosco, they are called to be "fathers and brothers" to the young. "If you want young people to grow," Don Bosco used to say, "you must not only love them: you must let them know they are loved."

Salesians live their lives in close contact with the young, sharing their life and interests while inviting them to Faith and Service. Through youth centers, parishes, schools, retreats and camps, Salesians help young people experience the loving presence of Jesus their Brother.

Formation Program

The formation program begins with the candidacy period, during or after high school. This program lasts two years and is followed by "Novitiate," which is a year of intense study of Salesian religious life.

After Novitiate, the candidate vows to live the gospel as a member of the Salesian family and continues his college program or goes on to further study.

Internship or "Practical Training" follows. This comprises two years of full-time ministry which allows the Salesian to experience the working community, deepen his commitment, and become adept in Don Bosco's educational methods.

Salesians who intend to become priests enter a four-year program in theology leading to a master's degree and ordination while those Salesians who are Brothers may choose a field of ministry or professional specialization and work towards a more in-depth qualification.

Specific Information

Salesian priests and Brothers form one community within Don Bosco's Salesian Family which includes other religious men and women, consecrated lay persons and dedicated young people. Their ministry is directed primarily to youth—especially the economically or spiritually disadvantaged.

Don Bosco's approach to life was one of joy and hard work. Salesians sustain their vital mission while trying to develop these same qualities in themselves. Youth respond to joy and the poor admire those who can work untiringly and selflessly on their behalf.

Salvatorians
Society of the Divine Savior

"A Life of Ministry and Leadership"

History/Charism

In answer to the needs of his time, Father Francis Jordan envisioned an institute of lay people who would carry the light of faith to areas where religious could not infiltrate. Through Jordan's efforts and activities, an institute calling itself the "Apostolic Teaching Society" was founded in 1881. This institute was an innovative and flexible group of people from all walks of life, e.g., lawyers, priests, laborers, scholars—each contributing his/her talents to spread the Word of God by any means possible.

As their work became more successful and their numbers grew, the institute evolved into a religious congregation known as the Society of the Divine Savior (Salvatorians). They spread throughout the United States, serving in parishes, schools, youth work, chaplaincies, home and foreign missions. At present, the 260 members of the American Province are found in over twenty states across the country, and in the African missions.

While we continue to serve in many and varied ministries, we have also expanded into sharing common Gospel ministries with lay men and women through the Salvatorian Associates, and researching new forms of ministry orientated toward the broader human community.

In a private audience, Jordan was given approval for his institute by Pope Leo XIII with these words: "If the work is in accord with the divine plan, it will succeed." In 1981, the Salvatorians celebrated and attested to their 100 years of success—bringing Christ back to contemporary society.

Ministry/Service

The Salvatorians do not specialize in one particular apostolate. The personnel policy within the Society in the U.S. has taken the direction of fulfilling the individual needs of the group to whom the individual ministers. Consequently, we are involved in many varied types of ministry: parish ministry, hospital chaplaincies, education, publishing, counseling centers, mental health, armed forces chaplains, college campus ministry, nursing homes, and many other areas.

Formation Program

New members grow into Salvatorian life through the following steps:

Contact Program: Men who are at least seniors in high school meet Salvatorians who invite them to participate in local community events and experiences.

Candidature: A six-month to two-year experience of living with other Salvatorians, sharing daily community life, and learning about our particular history and expression of religious life.

Novitiate: Novices wishing to study for the priesthood must be college graduates. Brother novices must have completed post high school training in their particular field. The novitiate is a year of in-depth examination of Salvatorian life, coupled with apostolic experiences. The novitiate year ends with the first profession of vows.

Temporary Commitment: A period of from three to nine years during which the Salvatorian may enter further studies, apostolic service, or a combination of both.

Specific Information

In the spirit of renewal the American Salvatorians expanded the membership of the Society. The inclusion of lay people in this expansion was then proposed in accordance with Father Jordan's original vision.

The intent of the experiment is to provide a structure within which mature Christian men and women who are willing to commit themselves to a life of ministry and leadership can seriously proceed to develop these roles in the Church.

The Scalabrinians
(Missionaries of St. Charles)

"Serving Migrants and Refugees for 100 Years"

History/Charism

Our founder, Bishop John Baptist Scalabrini (1839-1905) wanted us to be known as the Missionaries of St. Charles, but after his death people began calling us "Scalabrinians."

The words of the Lord *"I was a stranger and you took me into your home"* were for Bishop Scalabrini the missionary mandate he took at heart. Moved by the sad condition of migrants around the world, Scalabrini stirred up public opinion, the Church and the government to work for them. Therefore, in 1887 we were founded with the specific scope of caring for the spiritual and social welfare of migrants and refugees.

We number about 700 men and 900 women, living and working in small communities, scattered in 22 countries around the world. We share in common whatever we have and whatever we earn. We do not marry. We are ready to go wherever there are migrants and others forced to live outside their familiar environment, and who need the support of Christian faith. We seek to serve the unique Christ, who suffers injustice in work and services, fear, discrimination, loneliness from family separation and cultural conflict.

Ministry/Service

We Scalabrinians go to Christ in the migrants we serve by building new communities in the Amazonia of Brazil, by serving on the Vatican Commission for Migration and Tourism, by establishing Centers of Migration Studies around the world, by serving refugees in Tijuana, Paraguay and Uruguay.

In North America alone, you will find us with the Hispanic youth of a Chicago slum, the migrant worker of a California field, the Italian migrant of New England, the undocumented Haitian in a Brooklyn flat, and a Portuguese family in Vancouver.

Formation Program

Prenovitiate: You will be eligible to join our College Associate Program after your have completed High School. This program leads to a Bachelor of Arts or a Bachelor of Science Degree, with a minimum of six courses in Christian Systematic Philosophy in preparation for Theology. To broaden your ability to serve the migrants, sociology and the study of other languages will be part of your formation.

Novitiate: This period is the immediate and specific preparation for the complete gift of youself to Christ and the Church in our Scalabrinian community. You will be helped in your personal, Christian and religious growth, with particular regard to your future service to migrants and refugees.

Post-Novitiate: Having made your first religious profession, you will enter into the School of Theology, a three year program leading to the degree of Master of Divinity. This program will help you develop an understanding of your faith with pastoral wisdom and skills, that will enable you to exercise the ministry on behalf of migrants.

If you desire to join us as Brother, you will be helped with a theological, biblical and catechetical formation which will direct you toward the ministry of evangelization. You will also acquire professional skills in a chosen area so as to exercise a particular role entrusted to you on behalf of migrants.

After one year of Deacon Internship Program you will conclude your priestly preparation and the perpetual profession of the religious vows will make you a fully pledged member of the Scalabrinian community.

Servite Friars
The Order of Servants of Mary

"A Tradition of Fraternity, Mary and Service"

History/Charism

The Order of Friar Servants of Mary, commonly known as Servites, were founded in 1233 as an expression of evangelical apostolic life. We are an international community of priests and brothers gathered together in the name of Jesus the Lord.

Moved by the Spirit, we commit ourselves, as did our Seven Holy Founders, to witness the Gospel in fraternal communion and to be at the service of God's children, drawing inspiration from Mary, Mother and Servant of the Lord.

Ministry/Service

Following the traditional pattern of community life, our friars wish to manifest to the world around them the love which is theirs, to take on such apostolic work as is called for by the needs of the Church, to give new life to those which are characteristically Servite and to carry out all their work in brotherly harmony.

Friars engaged in parish ministry extend their brotherly love to others by establishing an ever growing community of faith which has its fullest expression in the Eucharistic assembly.

Friars engaged in education contribute to the intellectual and religious advancement of those to whom they minister.

Friars engaged in preaching and retreats are familiar with modern, concrete and contemporary methods.

Servite Friars also minister as hospital and military chaplains, counselors, administrators, foreign mission work and a variety of other apostolic works.

Formation Program

Candidates are accepted after the completion of high school or any time thereafter.

After college there is a year of spiritual and personal formation called novitiate. At the conclusion of the novitiate year the young friar professes the vows of poverty, chastity and obedience.

Theological preparation for ministry is pursued at Catholic Theological Union, Chicago, where for four years there is an ongoing academic, pastoral and spiritual formation program.

Religious formation is highlighted by the profession of solemn vows. If the friar is to be a cleric, ordination to the priesthood follows.

SONS of Mary, Missionaries

(Sons of Mary, Health of the Sick: F.M.S.I.)

History/Charism

When Jesus was asked by the emissaries of John the Baptist if he was the Messiah, his answer was to tell them what he was doing: "The blind see, the deaf hear, the lame walk, the leper is made clean, the dead are raised to life and the Good News is preached to the poor" (Mt. 11:4-5). We are the Sons of Mary, a missionary community of Christ's disciples in a lay religious Congregation dedicated to continuing the redemptive process begun by God in his living Covenant with his people. Ours is the ministry of healing, a ministry that defines health as a state of complete physical, mental, spiritual and social well-being, not merely the absence of disease or infirmity. We strive to live and work in such a way that those to whom we minister will know that God has acted upon them in a healing event.

Ministry/Service

It is our privilege to participate in the restoration of human harmony through our medical, catechetical and social apostolates. In our catechetical apostolate, we speak the Word to one another and to others around us. We train women and men in catechesis to evangelize and to teach others this work. In our medical apostolate, we treat the sick in body and spirit, as well as the social illnesses of our day: injustice, poverty, hunger and ignorance. In our social apostolate, we strive to identify ourselves with the aspirations of suffering people, actively promoting and participating in their liberation from misery.

The Sons of Mary, a missionary society of Brothers and priests, was founded in the Archdiocese of Boston in 1952 by Fr. Edward F. Garesche, a priest who devoted his whole life to the medical missionary work of the Church. We have just recently completed missionary programs in the jungles of Venezuela and in the inner-city slums of Lima, Peru and are now beginning a new mission in the Philippines. Our Brothers do missionary work in the US as well.

Specific Information

Young men attracted to the Sons of Mary usually have at least some college work completed, or have worked for some years after high school graduation. We look for men of strength, constancy, sacrificial spirit and a sense of humor who love God and his Blessed Mother and are zealous for the healing of bodies and souls to such an extent that they will forget themselves and work with untiring devotion to realize the spirit and vision of the Congregation. We look for men who want to give their whole lives to Jesus Christ and to the missionary service of his Church.

Spiritans

Congregation of the Holy Ghost

History/Charism

The Congregation of the Holy Ghost is an international community of 4000 priests and brothers committed to apostolic activity and education among peoples and groups whose material and spiritual needs are greatest and who are the most neglected—a service for which the Church has difficulty in finding apostolic workers. Although the priority is mission activity, the framework allows for various and diverse possibilities in education and specialized areas.

Claude Francois Poullart des Places in 1703, and Francis Libermann, a convert from Judaism in 1848, provided the impetus and dream for the Spiritans.

The Congregation was begun by Father des Places to provide adequate spiritual and academic preparation of students for the priesthood who came from impoverished backgrounds. The Holy Ghost Fathers and Brothers, also known as the Spiritans, soon became responsible for educating priests for the tremendous needs of the poor rural parishes in France and for the needs of all the French colonies. In 1848, Father Francis Libermann directed the Congregation to seek out those who, at the time, were the most impoverished in the terms of having heard the Good News. To the peoples of Africa, and peoples of African descent throughout the world, Francis Libermann committed legions of missionaries. The sons of Father Libermann began the modern evangelization of Africa and have numbered the most numerous of missionaries on that continent. Subsequent generations of Spiritans have expanded the mission to service in over sixty countries on six continents.

As a missionary, a Holy Ghost Father or Brother works to implant the Church or to renew it; he attempts to make a harmonious blend of the Church's religious tradition and the treasure of its literature, art and mysticism, with the nature and genius of the people he serves. He works for the glory of God, for service to the Church and the people of God, and for the betterment of the world through a concern for peace and justice.

Ministry/Service

A congregation that attempts to care for the forgotten of this world must become a complex combination of diversified personnel and resources, literally ready for everything.

From a home for neglected boys in Philadelphia to abandoned lepers in Africa; from a straw thatched school in Zaire to the illustrious French seminary in Rome and a modern university in Pittsburgh; from a string of orphanages in France to the development of Basic Christian Communities in the *favelas* of Brazil; from school in Ireland, Portugal and Trinidad to open-shirted dialogue with Massai warriors in East Africa; from helping renew the faith of Huastecan and Nahuatl Indians in the mountains of Mexico to sheltering Haitian refugees in Brooklyn; from the steaming jungles of central Africa to assisting the development of the Church in the Black and Hispanic communities in the United States—the Spiritan missionary will be found preaching the Gospel and developing the Church in areas where the need of committed and well-trained missionaries is the greatest. He is the bearer of Good News to the peoples the world most often overlooks or exploits.

Formation Program

Entrance into the Congregation can begin after initial contact through a non-residential association as an affiliate, while completing studies or other responsibilities in another area. During this time, frequent contact with the Spiritans and a retreat can lead the person toward a residential formation commitment. In the United States, college formation programs are centered at Duquesne Univeristy in Pittsburgh, PA., and University of St. Thomas in Houston, TX. The pre-novitiate program provides necessary orientation to missionary-religious life for those who have completed high school or have transferred from other colleges. Men who have completed collegiate studies are received into the pre-novititate programs for a period of at least one year. The novitiate is a one year experience of community and spiritual growth where one makes the decision to profess vows as a Spiritan missionary after reflecting on the history, tradition and goals of the Congregation. Our novitiate in Farnham, Quebec, is a common novitiate with Spiritan provinces of North America.

Following the novitiate, graduate studies in theology are pursued in Spiritan student communities at Catholic Theological Union in Chicago and the Oblate School of Theology in San Antonio, Texas. During these years a student is given the opportunity for a period of internship in a pastoral or missionary environment prior to ordination or final profession. Special attention is given to the particular talents and interests of individuals if they will enhance some dimension of his life and service in the congregation in its ministry and commitment to the poor.

If you are interested in sharing the Spiritan life and work as a priest or brother (candidates are accepted after high school, but normally not after age 40), please refer to the Index for names and locations of Spiritan Vocation Directors.

Specific Information

The Congregation feels specially blessed by the Holy Spirit for His guidance and renewing grace as it adapts its lifestyle to the needs of the historic Church and contemporary times. It has kept itself open to the dynamism of history and adapted itself to various situations in the Church among the diverse cultures of the nations which produce its Provinces and missions.

The Society of St. Sulpice

"A Ministry to Ministers"

History/Charism

The Society of St. Sulpice is a group of diocesan clergy dedicated to serving the priesthood. Their main work is the training of students for the diocesan priesthood and continuing education for priests and others involved in ministry.

The Society was founded in 1641 by Jean Jacques Olier, a parish priest in Paris. Realizing that the renewal of the Church depended upon renewal of its ministers, Fr. Olier was one of the first to implement successfully the decrees of the Council of Trent calling for the establishment of seminaries. As pastor of St. Sulpice, one of the largest and most active parishes in Paris, Fr. Olier attracted young candidates, and integrated a very practical training in pastoral service with theological training at the University, and an intensive development in prayer and spirituality.

The organization of the Society is unique. It functions much like a religious order, with canonically approved constitutions, a Superior General, and a centralized administration in each of the provinces. But in fact the Society is not a religious order. It is an institute for apostolic life whose members are diocesan priests who remain officially attached to their own diocese, while being freed by their bishops for the work of St. Sulpice.

Ministry/Service

Sulpicians are working in North and South America, Europe, Africa and Asia. The General Headquarters are in Paris, with the three Provinces centered in Paris, Montreal and Baltimore.

Sulpicians of the American Province serve over a hundred dioceses of the nation through regional seminaries and ministry training centers in Baltimore and Washington, D.C. on the East Coast, and in Menlo Park, Mountain View and Berkeley in California. Sulpicians also collaborate with diocesan offices for vocations and continuing education and other formation programs in several areas including Seattle, Honolulu, Wheeling and Santa Rosa. The three theologates integrate graduate programs in theology and professional programs in pastoral ministry with personal and spiritual formation, including spiritual direction and counseling and a rich liturgical life. A hallmark of these Sulpician programs has been the integration of faculty and students in a vital ecclesial community of faith and prayer. The college seminary is responding to present needs in the Church with its multi-ethnic programs. Sulpicians are increasingly active in providing different types of programs for deepening ministerial competence and spirituality for those already engaged in ministry. The Ecumenical Institute and the Institute for Continuing Education, both directed out of St. Mary's Seminary in Baltimore, offer rich resources from the Judaeo-Christian theological tradition to clergy and laity of all faiths and those involved in full time pastoral ministry. The Vatican II Institute located at St. Patrick's Seminary in Menlo Park, CA is currently directed by a Sulpician.

Many members of the Society are engaged in directing retreats for priests, religious, and the laity and in giving workshops in theology, scripture, religious education, homiletics and other ministry-oriented areas.

Formation Program

Candidates to the Society come from the ranks of diocesan clergy. However, seminarians, graduate students who might be considering priesthood as a vocation, and other laymen, qualified and free to pursue this special ministry as priests are encouraged to inquire. After ordination, candidates serve in their dioceses for at least two years. Upon release from their dioceses they are normally assigned to a Sulpician institution for two years. There follows a year of special Sulpician formation and a summer session in Paris with young Sulpicians from around the world. Depending on the circumstances, candidates are then encouraged to pursue postgraduate studies in theology, scripture, spirituality, pastoral care or other specialized areas. Once they complete their graduate work they are assigned to a Sulpician program and are eligible to apply for definitive membership.

Trappists
New Melleray Abbey
Cistercian Monks

"A Life Hidden in Christ"

History/Charism

New Melleray Abbey was founded 130 years ago by monks from Mount Melleray in Ireland. It is situated in the rolling farmland of northeastern Iowa, 12 miles from Dubuque.

The monks of New Melleray Abbey are men totally dedicated to contemplation. "Our life is humility, voluntary poverty, obedience, peace and joy in the Holy Spirit. It is submission to a master, to an abbot, to a Rule, and to a discipline. It is application to silence, the practice of fasting and vigils, the exercise of prayer and manual labor. Above all it consists in following the most excellent of ways which is that of charity" (St. Bernard, Letter 142).

Ministry/Service

The mission and ministry of the Cistercian monk in the world today is contemplative presence. The Pilgrim Church is missionary by her very nature because of the fountain of love which springs up in her heart desiring that all people be saved and come to share in the life of God. As monks totally dedicated to contemplation, we share in this missionary activity of the Church not by an active apostolate, but by prayer, works of penance, and sufferings for the evangelization of the whole world. And because the contemplative life belongs to the fullness of the Church's presence, we desire the growth and expansion of monastic life so that new communities may be established everywhere.

Formation Program

Men who seek to enter our community are encouraged to visit New Melleray Abbey. Serious candidates are given the opportunity to live within the community for several weeks to become acquainted with our monastic way of life. This period of observership will assist the candidate in discerning his vocation. He always returns to his home for a month or more before he may apply for entrance into the monastery as a postulant. The postulancy lasts about six months, followed by a two year novitiate. Then temporary vows or promises from three to six years lead up to Solemn Profession and full membership in the community. Some of the monks go on to become priests depending on the needs of the community and the particular vocation of the individual.

Specific Information

The monks rise at 3:15 a.m. Throughout the day they seek God continuously by communal and private prayer, sacred reading, and manual labor. Farming provides the principal means of self support. All the monks, except the infirm, abstain from meat. At 8:00 p.m. they retire for the night.

Men who have finished high school and worked for a few years, or completed college education may apply for entrance to our contemplative way of life.

Trinity Missions
Missionary Servants of the Most Holy Trinity

"Missions Are People"

History/Charism

We are a young religious community in the Catholic Church. We were founded in 1929, here in the United States—in the backwoods of Alabama—by Father Thomas Judge.

Father Judge, a Vincentian priest, did not intend to start a religious community when he began his ministry. He was concerned about the tremendous "leakage" from the Church, especially among recent Catholic immigrants. He realized that religious and clergy could not meet this challenge by themselves. An apostolic laity was needed to meet these people where they lived and worked. In 1909 in Brooklyn, Father Judge gathered his first band of laity and challenged them to become apostles. As he traveled, he established more of these groups which he called "Cenacles" (a word that means upper room—reminiscent of the upper room in which the first apostles were taught, nourished and commissioned by Jesus). By 1915, he had organized several hundred lay apostles.

That year, Father Judge was assigned to a mission parish in Alabama. Soon many lay people joined him and began to visit the homes of the urban and rural poor, ministering to their spiritual as well as physical needs.

From these lay missionaries and volunteers, two religious communities came into being. The Missionary Servants of the Most Holy Trinity was established for the men called to be priests or Brothers. The Missionary Servants of the Most Blessed Trinity was established for the women called to be Sisters. And those laity called to be lay apostles were known as the Missionary Cenacle Apostolate. And so we are a religious family of priests, Brothers and Sisters.

Ministry/Service

As a religious community, we continue to respond to the challenge of Father Judge's inspiration. We are missionaries to those in danger of losing the Faith—especially the materially poor and spiritually abandoned. We strive to help develop the ministries and apostleship of every Catholic lay person. We seek to serve on the missions as a family of priests, Brothers, Sisters, and laity.

These aims have carried us to the inner cities, the rural South, the Alaska wilderness, the Appalachian mountains, the barrios and special ministries throughout the United States, as well as the villages and towns in Puerto Rico and Mexico. We truly believe—Missions are People!

Formation Program

Our formation programs are varied in the pre-novitiate phase, depending on college preparation and age of our candidates. The novitiate is a one year experience of our charism and spirituality. The post-novitiate formation, from three to five years until final vows, is varied depending on the particular preparation for ministry. Throughout this formation process, periodic service on the missions is expected of each person.

Order of the Most Holy Trinity
The Trinitarians

"Seeking Freedom and Dignity for Captive Christians"

History/Charism

Red, white and blue stood for freedom long before people knew North America existed. They became the symbols of freedom in 1198 when St. John DeMatha and a band of men first wore the habit of the Trinitarians—a white habit with a red and blue cross. Begun in the wake of the Crusades, St. John DeMatha conceived the idea of a new religious order whose purpose would be the ransoming of captive Christians held in slavery by the Moslems. The earliest friars begged, bribed, performed espionage work and even traded themselves into slavery to secure the freedom of others.

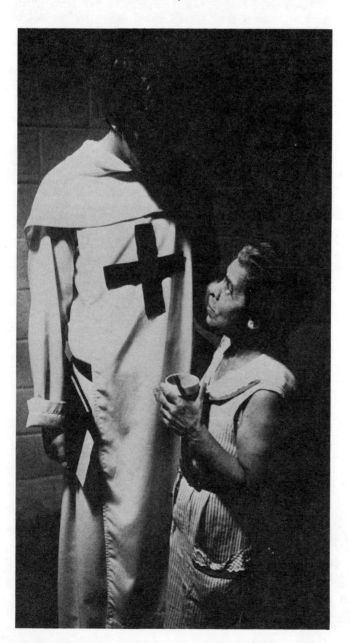

The lifestyle of the friars was unique for its time in that it combined the best elements of both the active and contemplative life.

During the first 500 years the Order grew rapidly throughout Europe as the friars continued their ransoming work, freeing thousands of captive Christians and establishing hospices to care for them upon their release. Among the many notable men and women involved with the Trinitarians during that time was Cervantes, the great spanish writer of *Don Quixote*. He was taken captive for five years and finally freed by the Trinitarians. Thomas Jefferson, as French ambassador also employed the aid of Trinitarian friars to free 119 American seaman captured by Barbary Pirates. In the sixteenth century it was the Trinitarians that accompanied the historic voyages of Vasco da Gama, DeSoto and Cortez in bringing the faith to the New World.

Ministry/Service

As our church and society change, so do the needs of people. We remain open to these new challenges of modern captivity by working for social justice and human dignity of the poor, the street people, the juvenile delinquent, the prisoner, the sick and terminally ill, the retarded and emotionally ill, and those in mission territories that are most in need. Today there remain thousands held captive for their Christian beliefs, and the Trinitarians have adapted to their times by working with international organizations for the release of these captives. Our European friars have even been known to smuggle literature and supplies to those in communist countries. As Trinitarians we feel called to bring the gospel message of freedom where it is needed the most, so we are an international religious order located throughout the world.

Formation Program

Men interested in entering the Trinitarians to become a priest or brother must have a minimum of two years of college education. At that time they would enter our Affiliate Program, living as single men with our community while they complete their undergraduate education. There is no commitment on their part to the Order, and they are free to leave at anytime. Upon completion of this program, they may request admission to the Novitiate. The Novitiate program lasts one year, at which time the friar would take temporary vows of poverty, chastity and obedience. He remains in temporary vows for a minimum of three years while he pursues theological studies in Washington, D.C. At the end of the period of temporary vows the friar may make his lifetime commitment to the Order through Solemn Vows. Following this the friar could choose ordination to the priesthood and begin his ministerial work, or may elect to continue his education in a specific field of study.

Specific Information

The United States Province of the Order of the Most Holy Trinity embraces the entire country. We have two monasteries, one in Baltimore and the other in Washington, D.C., but generally live in smaller and more intimate communities. While we are an old Order in the church, we are a young province in the United States. Our median age for the men in our province is 35. We work together as priests and brothers. We are unconventional in our methods and modern in our monasticism.

The Viatorians
The Clerics of St. Viator

"Helping Others To Follow Christ"

History/Charism

The Viatorians, besides doing their best to live the Gospel among themselves, have two main concerns. One is helping people to build a faith in Christ that is intelligent and life-giving. The other is bringing people together to celebrate their lives and faith in ways that move them to reach beyond themselves to the needs of others. Viatorians are predominantly teachers and parish ministers, therefore, who place a high value on taking people "where they are" and helping them to live their faith infectiously in the real world.

This international community of brothers, deacons and priests got its start in France just a century and a half ago. It began as a lay association whose members offered the then unique and urgent service of being general parish assistants and organizers as well as professional teachers of religion and the three "R's."

Today, Viatorians continue to pursue professionalism in secular as well as religious studies and pursuits. This kind of training, they believe, keeps them faithful to their origins. It also prepares them well to live their faith in the real world, to understand, interpret and evaluate contemporary society in the light of faith, and to help those they serve do the same.

Ministry/Service

Viatorians concentrate their efforts primarily in high schools and parishes. However, they are also significantly involved in parish grade schools, CCD programs, youth ministries, and college and adult education as teachers, administrators, counselors, advisors, and pastoral ministers.

Hospital chaplaincy is a strong secondary ministry. Other areas of service are open to the members through individual request.

Formation Program

Viatorians offer a non-residency contact program of suggested readings, spiritual guidance and vocation awareness weekends. A residency Affiliate program for twenty to forty year olds offers an opportunity to experience Viatorian community life while attending college or pursuing their chosen work or profession. This program focuses on personal identity, skills for creative group living, faith development, and vocational choice. The next stage is a one year Novitiate that concentrates on spiritual growth and preparation for life and ministry as a Viatorian. After Novitiate, temporary vows are made for three years and may be renewed for up to nine years before making a final commitment.

Priesthood candidates attend Catholic Theological Union in Chicago. Brothers pursue advanced studies or training at various institutions. Life-long professional development is strongly encouraged.

Specific Information

The Viatorians have approximately 150 members living and working primarily in Illinois and Las Vegas, Nevada. They live mostly in small groups and stress collaboration with others at all levels of their life and work.

College students who join the Viatorian affiliate program are expected to pay their own expenses and tuition. Room and board are nominal. Most affiliates help finance their education with summer jobs. Financial aid is available to those who need it.

Vincentian Priests and Brothers
Congregation of the Mission

"Bringing the Gospel to the Poor"

History/Charism

St. Vincent de Paul was a truly Christ-like priest, a warm-hearted man with unbounded love for people, especially the poor, the oppressed, the neglected. St. Vincent spent most of his priestly life ministering to the needs of sick people, the poor, the hungry, convicts, and the galley slaves. He preached, taught, fed, healed, and liberated them.

In 1625, St. Vincent founded an Institute of priests, the Congregation of the Mission, to assist him in his work. Today, the Congregation of the Mission, as a religious community of priests and brothers, has a world membership of approximately 4300. In the United States, there are about 700 priests, 50 brothers, and 160 candidates. These Vincentians are missionaries, teachers, preachers, parish priests, chaplains, and spiritual directors.

Ministry/Service

Many Vincentians are engaged in direct work with the poor serving in parishes throughout the United States, as well as in Panama, Taiwan, Africa and Guatemala. Other Vincentians are involved in the formation of the clergy. They conduct seminaries for the formation of the diocesan clergy, as well as their own Vincentian candidates in Northampton, St. Louis, Denver, and Los Angeles. Still others are engaged in university education and administration. The Vincentians administer three universities: St. John's University, Niagara University, and DePaul University. Vincentians serve as chaplains in hospitals, prisons, and in the armed forces. They are on mission bands, conduct retreats and Miraculous Medal novenas, and have home missions.

It is because of these works that candidates for the Vincentians must have sufficient academic ability to follow a demanding course of studies. They should be able to earn a bachelor's degree and to do graduate work especially in theology.

Formation Program

The program of formation consists of four parts: high school, college, novitiate, and theological study. The program varies for the five provinces of the Vincentians in the United States, but each has these common elements. For those who seek to enter the Vincentians later in life, each case is reviewed on an individual basis when the candidate applies for admission to the Congregation.

In addition to the priests, there are also Vincentians who are Brothers. These are men who seek to follow St. Vincent and his example by living a vowed life, but do not seek ordination. Brothers in the Vincentian Community perform many ministries such as teaching, working with the poor, manual labor, administration, etc. They follow a formation program geared especially for them, with some college work required.

Specific Information

Those who enter the Vincentian Community take vows of poverty, chastity and obedience. The vow of poverty is a profession to be poor in spirit and in fact, both individually and communally. The vow of chastity is a promise to willingly give up being married so as to be able to love universally. The vow of obedience is a faithful response to the decisions of the superiors and the needs of the Community in matters that affect the common good.

Vocationist Fathers

"Vocations Are Our Business"

History/Charism

The Society of Divine Vocations, whose members are known as Vocationist Fathers and Brothers, is a modern religious community with the three vows of Poverty, Chastity and Obedience.

The Community was founded in Naples, Italy, in 1920, by the Ven. Servant of God, Fr. Justin Russolillo, who died in Pianura of Naples on August 2, 1955. The idea of working for vocations and the foundation of the Congregation was the ultimate goal of Fr. Justin's life. "The Congregation was born with me," he used to say.

On September 20, 1913, Justin was ordained a priest. At that time Pope Pius X had made a fervent appeal to promote a greater interest in vocations. The appeal made its way into the generous heart of Fr. Justin. He decided to devote every moment of his life and all his energies toward the fulfillment of the Holy Father's desire and the Church's dire need as well. His plans were interrupted by the First World War, but after the war Fr. Justin came with a fervent desire to make his dream come true.

Appointed Pastor of Pianura on September 20, 1920, he soon started working for the realization of his mission. On October 18th of the same year, the Community of the Vocationist Fathers came into being. The Community received final Papal approval on January 18, 1968.

Ministry/Service

In the United States, the Vocationist Fathers are relatively new, coming here in 1962. While here in the United States, the focus has been mostly in parish work, while the foundation was being laid for the true vocational apostolate. Now, after 20 years, the Vocationist Fathers are ready to fully assume their vocational work.

The search and cultivation of vocations, especially among the poor and underprivileged, is the specific goal of the Vocationist Fathers. They have special formation institutions called VOCATIONARIES in which they gather all those who show signs of vocations, and through a life of prayer, study and sacrifice, help them to ascertain their vocation first, and then assist them in selecting a Diocese or a Religious Order.

The Vocationist Fathers believe that every person has a vocation in life, and that each individual finds complete self-fulfillment and success only in the pursuit of his own vocation. While consecrating their efforts to vocations to Priesthood and Religious Life, they dedicate themselves also to assisting each person in responding to the general vocation to life, to faith, to holiness and to every individual's vocation in life.

In addition to their work in the Vocationaries, the Vocationist Fathers serve the people of God also in parishes, schools, missions and wherever there is an individual trying to identify and follow his calling in life.

Formation Program

Interested men who are desiring to visit the community are welcome at any time. The main requirements for admission to the community are: an attraction to God, a willingness to serve His people and a strong desire to become a saint. A high school diploma is also required.

Once someone is admitted to the community, he will undergo a postulancy period in order to adjust to community life. Then begins the novitiate period which lasts for one year. During this year the novice will learn about prayer life, the Vocationist spirit and the vows of poverty, chastity and obedience. Apostolic work is also a part of the novitiate. After the novitiate, he makes the profession of the vows which are made temporarily for three years

before they become perpetual. It is at this point that the individual must consider as addressed to himself the words of Hosea, "I will make you my spouse forever." For those pursuing priesthood, a college degree and four years of theological studies are required for ordination.

Members of the Vocationist Fathers continue in the formation process throughout their life tending toward the ultimate purpose of every vocation which is divine union with the Most Holy Trinity.

Specific Information

The Vocationist Fathers are in four countries at the present time: Italy, Brazil, Argentina and the United States. In these countries they work in parishes, schools, missions and vocational work. In the United States the Vocationist Fathers work in the dioceses of Newark, New Jersey and Harrisburg, Pennsylvania.

Wherever they work, they carry on the spirit of Fr. Justin Russolillo, the Founder. He spent his life in prayer and service to God. He practiced every kind of spiritual and physical mortification, but he always admonished his religious not to indulge in physical privations by saying the great mortification of a Vocationist consists of "modesty and continuous work." And what better service for a man to give, as Fr. Justin did, than to live a sincere, priestly and religious vocation, always encouraging those who also want to serve.

Xaverian Missionaries

"Total Commitment to Foreign Missions"

History/Charism

Francis Xavier became a saint because he cared enough to get involved. He came to realize an almost impossible dream, the beginning of the conversion to Christ of the great nations of the Orient.

Xaverian priests and brothers have adopted Francis Xavier as their ideal: they strive to excel both as foreign missionaries and as messengers of the Gospel of God's love to all mankind.

Ministry/Service

Today Xaverians joyfully man some of the toughest foreign missions in the world. In the Far East they work for the "Greater Glory of Christ" in Bangladesh, on the island of Sumatra and in the Mentawai Islands of Indonesia and on the Japanese Islands of Kyushu, Honshu and Tanegashima.

In Africa, Xaverians work among the tribes of southwest Zaire, Burundi, and Sierra Leone.

In Latin America, Xaverian missions are located in the 'pampas' of south-central Brazil, as well as along Brazil's Amazon River, on the Buenaventura shores of Colombia and among the Indians in central Mexico.

Whether it be Asia, Africa or Latin America, Xaverian priests and brothers work in small groups and give witness of Christ's love through their brotherly love and prayer-life and also by becoming active in community-building, teaching, health care and social work.

Formation Program

Those interested in sharing the Xaverian way of life must have graduated from high school and be not older than 35 years of age. Since the work and way of life can be demanding, good physical and mental health are important considerations. Most of all, they must be willing to accept the challenge of the foreign missions with great faith, hope and love.

Specific Information

Whether the Xaverian missionary works among Moslems, Buddhists, Shintoists or people whose faith is the belief of their tribe, the American Xaverians may well be working side by side with Xaverians from Brazil, England, Italy, Mexico, Scotland or Spain. Together they form the Xaverian Family, bound together not only by the common mission in life and missionary enthusiasm, but also by a way of life sustained by vows of poverty, love, loyalty and a life-long and exclusive commitment to the foreign missions.

Discernment Resources

"Speak, Lord, Your Servant Is Listening"

1 Samuel 3:10

A Special Word...
...to Those Considering
Ministries for the Lord

Many are the challenges and rewards as well as obstacles and influences to consider in assessing whether you want to choose one of the ministries for the Lord as a priest, brother or deacon for your life's work.

You'll find the material that follows helpful for your vocational search and self-appraisal into Church vocation.

In the following pages, there is material to help you in your daily search into the question of HOW GOD IS CALLING YOU! We urge you to pray daily for your vocational direction. A prayer card is provided on the information card page at the end of this book.

If in your discernment and searching you opt to do so, contact the vocation director of the religious community in which you are interested. The addresses are in the directory. Or you may wish to use one of the cards at the back of this book (especially if you wish to contact more than one community). Contacting your local diocesan vocation director is a very helpful step also.

Thus, we encourage you to "BE A DOER, NOT ONLY A HEARER OF THE WORD." (James 1:22)

Six, Maybe Seven Ways to Grow

"Ways" are options. Have them your way. There is nothing sacred about the numerical order. Start with four; jump to one; switch to six; revamp the process; change the how-to-do-it. Create your own formula for growth and then maybe grow out of it or find in it a long-time pattern.

1. Relax

Before a person can learn to relax mentally, he needs to learn to relax physically. Find a quiet place.

Stretch and get comfortable. Take a deep breath...hold it...and as you slowly exhale feel yourself relaxing. Take another deep breath...hold it...flex and tighten the muscles of your hands, arms, shoulders...hold it...slowly exhale and relax these limbs.

Take another deep breath...hold it and flex the muscles in your feet, legs, buttocks...as you slowly exhale relax these parts of your body.

Take another deep breath...flex your entire body for a moment or two...as you slowly exhale, let your entire body go. You will feel your body growing lighter as all the tensions disappear.

Take another deep breath...hold it...as you slowly exhale feel a wave of relaxation sweep slowly down your body from the top of your head right out through the soles of your feet. The tension is leaving...

You are now in complete charge of the relaxation of your body. You can relax any part of your body at will. Relax...relax...

Observe your breathing. Don't change it, just observe it...Is your breathing smooth? If it is jerky, slowly even it out...Is your breathing rapid? If so, gradually slow it down...Close your eyes and try to establish a pattern of slow, deep, even breathing.

When you are relaxed, when your body is at peace, you are better able to think clearly, to understand your feelings, to listen to your deepest self. Relax...

2. Keep a Journal

Writing in a journal is a personal tool for growth, for personal integration, and for the development of awareness, as well as for getting in touch with the flow of one's life. As a tool it should be used by those who feel comfortable with it, and should be used when needed. Many find it useful when there is a "problem"—an important question to be dealt with, a time of difficulty, a need to understand feelings a bit better.

A journal is personal. We can work in it not only *when* we wish, but also in the *depth* we wish. There are some things we will feel uneasy in writing; in that case, we do not write them—we wait. We write when we are comfortable in doing so. No one rushes us with our journal; there is no pace we have to keep. It is our tool.

Some general ideas about writing in a journal include the following;

1. Always date the entry; when you re-read the journal, the date may be important.
2. Always write for yourself; never write with the intention of showing the journal to anyone else. Although you may later want to share it with someone close to you, do not write with the intention of doing so.
3. Always write descriptively and non-judgmentally; just write what you feel regardless of whether it looks "right" or "wrong."
4. Don't erase. If you wish to add or nuance, do so, but don't erase.
5. After you have finished an entry, re-read it, then add how you feel now that you have re-read what you have written.

What can you write about? You might want to write about important events in your life or feelings you would like to understand a little better; you might dialogue with yourself—trying to "argue" both sides of a decision; you might dialogue with another person or consider your future—just about anything. Writing helps you organize and sort through your feelings. It takes a while to get the "feel" for journal writing—so stay with it. It's worth it.

3. Choose a Guide

None of us can go it alone. If we are interested in advancing in our Christian journey, we may benefit from enlisting a guide.

Choose someone you feel is farther along the road and heading in the direction you wish to go. This friend is someone you can comfortably talk with, someone who will listen. He or she is not a mother or father substitute, not the perfect Christian, not the one with all the answers. This guide is someone whose experience and empathy allow you to tell your story, look at yourself honestly and gain some direction.

Through such a relationship, a person comes to know himself better, to realize some of the possibilities ahead and some ways to proceed. A certain amount of stagnation can be avoided, pitfalls side-stepped, self-deception surfaced, and self-doubt overcome.

Choosing a guide can be one of the wisest things a person does. Meeting regularly with this guide can help bring out the best in anyone serious about growing in the Christian life.

4. Read/Meditate

Many people find meditative reading to be a very helpful way to gain deeper insight into themselves. This is not textbook reading; it is slow, thoughtful, deep reading. It is sometimes helpful to begin with some form of the relaxing exercises mentioned earlier.

The "method" of meditative reading involves three simple steps:
• reading a line or phrase at a time.
• applying it to your life,
• and, for some, praying about it.

The book or material you select for meditative reading should be rich in content. Some of the best material includes thought provoking sections from novels, plays, essays, inspirational prayers, and poetry as well as passages from the Scriptures.

The important thing about meditative reading is not to hurry or to attempt to read too much at one time. Some people only read a line or two per day but this provides them plenty of material upon which to reflect. The reading is not as important as the application of what you have read to your own life. How do you see yourself in what you have read? Does this passage "speak" to you?

Some people use meditative reading as a method of prayer. By taking time to relax, to be reflective, they find that this type of reading—particularly when it is from Scripture—puts them in the "mood" for dialogue with God.

Try some of these:
"Thy will be done."
"No servant can be the slave of two masters."
"Your Father, who sees what you do in private, will reward you."
"Lord, make me an instrument of your peace."

5. Pray

What, you ask, is prayer? By prayer is meant the opening of your mind and heart to the mystery of God's role in existence, and especially in your personal existence. To pray means to be open to God in whatever form He may come to you, and to respond to His coming. Therefore, you must be alert to His coming in creation or nature, to His approach in the words in Scripture, or to His word made flesh in the Eucharist or in the suffering, need, or joy of one of your brothers or sisters in the world. If you are not to be blind to His coming, you must be open, aware, reflective, and responsible—that is, have the ability to respond to God.

For many persons, the tools for reflective living that have been mentioned so far—dialogue, the journal, meditative reading, bodily and mental relaxation—are all aids, or forms of prayer. Each tool is helpful to the extent that it makes you more reflective, more open, more responsive to the presence of God in your life.

Here are some thoughts about entering into prayer:
1. Find a suitable place—free from distractions.
2. Realize that harmony of body and spirit is important; take a peaceful, relaxed position.
3. Spend a few moments quieting yourself as you come into the presence of the Lord, believing He is with you.
4. Be a receptive listener—prayer is primarily LISTENING, not talking to God.
5. Reflect on what God has said to you.
6. Respond in simplicity and honesty.

A humble attitude of listening is a sign of love for Him, and a real prayer from the heart. Speak, Lord, your servant is listening. (1 Samuel 3:10)

6. Serve

Peter Maurin, co-founder of the Catholic Worker movement, used to encourage his listeners to be "go-givers." This giving-without-reserve is at the heart of the gospel message. Service is the cornerstone of Christian living.

Give and it shall be given to you. Whoever would gain his or her life must give it away. Anyone among you who aspires to greatness must serve the rest; whoever wants to rank first among you must serve the rest.

The big world out there—our city, country, world—is full of need. Our little world—family, friends, fellow students and fellow workers—is full of need. We give life and find life in serving those around us. Life expects something different from each of us. We pray, listen, and take chances to discover our own ways of responding.

One person is active in Bread for the World, another does shopping for a shut-in neighbor; one volunteers to tutor students needing help, another coaches the sixth grade basketball team; one teaches skills at the center for retarded adults, another spends a summer building homes in Appalachia. One or another, each finds his or her own ways to serve.

As we have been given, so we are to give in return. And there is growth in giving.

7. Consider

If you remember, the title read: "Six, maybe seven ways to grow." Well, we have suggested six ways that can help you grow.

Now, for some of you, we offer a seventh possible way to grow—as a brother, priest, deacon, or lay minister.

If you are the type of person for whom a reflective life of service is important, the kind of person who is looking for ways to deepen your own growth and who is interested in developing your ability to promote and enhance that same type of growth in others—then you might be the type of person to consider a Church vocation.

Ask yourself what is most important in your life. How interested are you in your own growth, the growth and well-being of others? Are you looking for creative and meaningful ways to live your life, to help others live?

In fact, you might want to use some of the methods in this booklet—the journal, dialogue, prayer, and the others. Each method is a different way of listening; each may yield something a bit different. Try them. Think about this seventh one...

Adapted from the booklet by Bro. Tom Collins, Brothers of the Christian Schools.

Reprinted with permission from:
National Catholic Vocation Council

Copies of SIX, MAYBE SEVEN WAYS TO GROW available from:

1307 South Wabash Ave. #350
Chicago, IL 60605
312/663-5453

Readings for Discernment

Bausch, William, UNDERSTANDING THE SACRAMENTS (Fides)

Carroll, L. Patrick, TO LOVE, TO SHARE, TO SERVE: CHALLENGES TO A RELIGIOUS (Liturgical Press)

Champlin, Joseph M. BEHIND CLOSED DOORS: A Handbook on How to Pray (Paulist)

Green, Thomas, WEEDS AMONG WHEAT: Discernment Where Prayer and Action Meet (Ave Maria Press)

Hakenwerth, Quentin, SM, FOLLOWING YOUR INNER CALL: A Decision-making Process Workbook (National Catholic Vocation Council)

Hellwig, Monika, UNDERSTANDING CATHOLICISM (Paulist)

Kavanaugh, J.F., FOLLOWING CHRIST IN A CONSUMER SOCIETY (Orbis)

Metz, Johannes B., FOLLOWERS OF CHRIST: Perspectives on Religious Life (Paulist)

National Catholic Vocation Council, Lifestyle/Ministry Booklet Series, TO BROTHER, RELIGIOUS PRIEST, LAY MINISTER, SISTER, DIOCESAN PRIEST, MISSIONARY (National Catholic Vocation Council)

Nolan, Albert, JESUS BEFORE CHRISTIANITY (Orbis)

Pable, Martin, OFM, Cap., A CALL FOR ME (Sunday Visitor)

Pennington, M. Basil, CALLED: New Thinking on Christian Vocation (Seabury Press)

Perkins, Pheme, READING THE NEW TESTAMENT (Paulist)

Schmidt, Joseph F., FSC, PRAYING OUR EXPERIENCES (St. Mary's Press)

Simon, Arthur, BREAD FOR THE WORLD (Paulist)

Whitehead, E.E. and J.D. Whitehead, CHRISTIAN LIFE PATTERNS (Doubleday)

Additional Vocation Resources

A basic contact is your local diocesan vocation office. The following national offices may have further information.

ASSOCIATION OF PERMANENT
  DIACONATE DIRECTORS (APUD)
1200 Varnum Street, NE
Washington, DC 20017

INTERNATIONAL LIAISON FOR
  VOLUNTEER SERVICES INC.
1234 Massachusetts Ave., NW
Washington, DC 20005

NATIONAL ASSEMBLY OF
  RELIGIOUS BROTHERS (NARB)
1307 S. Wabash 2nd Fl
Chicago, IL 60605

NATIONAL CONFERENCE OF
  DIOCESAN VOCATION DIRECTORS
1307 S. Wabash #350
Chicago, IL 60605

NATIONAL CONFERENCE OF
  RELIGIOUS VOCATION DIRECTORS
1307 S. Wabash #350
Chicago, IL 60605

NATIONAL CATHOLIC VOCATION
  COUNCIL
1307 S. Wabash #350
Chicago, IL 60605

NATIONAL OFFICE OF BLACK
  CATHOLICS (NOBC)
1234 Massachusetts Ave., NW #1004
Washington, DC 20005

PADRES
3310 Garfield
Kansas City, KS 66104

SECRETARIAT FOR HISPANIC AFFAIRS
1312 Massachusetts Ave., NW
Washington, DC 20005

SERRA INTERNATIONAL
22 West Monroe St.
Chicago, IL 60603

TEKAKWITHA CONFERENCE
1818 9th Avenue So., #5
Great Falls, MT 59405

U.S. CONFERENCE OF SECULAR
  INSTITUTES
7007 Bradley Blvd.
Bethesda, MD 20034

Index of Communities

Index of
Vocation Directors

SOCIETY OF AFRICAN MISSIONS

Rev. Joseph F. Foley, SMA
269 Common Street
Dedham, MA 02026
617-326-2512

Vocation Director, SMA
6256 N. Newcastle Ave.
Chicago, IL 60631
312-775-5050

SOCIETY OF MISSIONARIES OF AFRICA

Office of Mission, Recruitment
2020 W. Morse Avenue
Chicago, IL 60645

Provincial Headquarters
1624 21st St., NW
Washington, DC 20009

ALEXIAN BROTHERS

Br. David Witalka, CFA
600 Alexian Way
Elk Grove Village, IL 60007
312-981-3625

Br. Reginald Gleasure, CFA
225 N. Jackson Avenue
San Jose, CA 95116
408-259-5000

ASSUMPTIONISTS

Vocation Director, AA
364 Buckminister Road
Brookline, MA 02146
617-731-3380

SOCIETY OF THE ATONEMENT

Vocation Office
1925 N. Berendo Street
Los Angeles, CA 90027
213-660-7734

Vocation Office
Graymoor
Garrison, NY 10524
914-424-3671

Vocation Office
St. Anthony Church
115 N. Twenty-five Mile Ave.
Hereford, TX 79045
806-364-6150

Vocation Office
St. Joseph the Worker Church
4451 Williams Road
Richmond, BC V7E 1J7
CANADA
604-277-8353

Vocation Office
Church of the Atonement
2940 Forest Glade Drive
Windsor, ONT N8R 1L5
CANADA
519-735-6023

AUGUSTINIAN RECOLLECTS

Rev. Jose J. Mendez, OAR
San Miguel Church
2214 E. 108th St.
Los Angeles, CA 90059
213-569-5951
213-567-1850

Rev. Allen J. Hill, OAR
Tagaste Monastery
Suffern, NY 10901
914-357-0067

AUGUSTINIANS

Vocation Office
Austin House
1605 28th Street
San Diego, CA 92102
619-233-9141

Vocation Office
P.O. Box 338
Villanova, PA 19085
215-645-7595

Vocation Office
20300 Governors Hwy.
Olympia Fields, IL 60461
312-748-9500

Vocation Office
Good Counsel Vice Province
St. Augustine Prep
Richland, NY 08350
609-697-2600

BARNABITES

Rev. Richard F. Kammerer, CRSP
Dewberry & Madison Avenues
Bethlehem, PA 18017
215-691-8648

BASILIAN FATHERS

Vocation Director
95 St. Joseph Street
Toronto, ONT M5S 2R9
CANADA
416-925-4368

Rev. Dennis P. Noelke, CSB
402 Augustine Street
Rochester, NY 14613
716-458-6471

BENEDICTINES

Rev. Becket G. Senchur, OSB
St. Vincent Archabbey
Latrobe, PA 15650
412-539-9761

*Rev. Aelred Cody, OSB
St. Meinrad Archabbey
St. Meinrad, IN 47577
812-357-6611

*Rev. Christopher R. Schwartz, OSB
2900 King Drive
Cleveland, OH 44104
216-721-5300

*Rev. Theodore Suchy, OSB
St. Procopius Abbey
5601 College Road
Lisle, IL 60532
312-969-6410

Rev. Bruce Swift, OSB
St. Benedict's Abbey
Atchison, KS 66002
913-367-5340

Vocation Director, OSB
St. Anselm Abbey
Manchester, NH 03102
603-669-1030

Vocation Director, OSB
Woodside Priory
302 Portola Road
Portola Valley, CA 94025
415-851-8220

Vocation Director, OSB
Belmont Abbey
Belmont, NC 28012
704-825-3711

Vocation Director, OSB
Conception Abbey
Conception, MO 64433
816-944-2211

Vocation Director, OSB
Glastonbury Abbey
16 Hull Street
Hingham, MA 02043
617-749-2155

Rev. Ralph Wright, OSB
St. Louis Priory
500 S. Mason Road
St. Louis, MO 63141

Vocation Director
St. Benedict's Abbey
Benet Lake, WI 53102
414-396-4311

CONGREGATION OF THE
BLESSED SACRAMENT

Br. Robert Zeegers, SSS
1335 W. Harrison Street
Chicago, IL 60607
312-243-7400

CAMALDOLESE MONKS

Rev. Victor Atkocaitis, Cam., OSB
Immaculate Heart Hermitage
Big Sur, CA 93920
408-667-2456

CARMELITES

St. Elias Province
Rev. Francis M. Amodio, O.Carm.
57 Lincoln Avenue
Box 127
Purchase, NY 10577
212-679-1421

Most Pure Heart of Mary Province
Rev. Chris I. Pieklo, O. Carm.
6343 N. Wayne Ave.
Chicago, IL 60660
312-973-2740

Rev. Charles Francis Kurgan, O. Carm.
1540 East Glenn
Tucson, AZ 85719
602-325-1537

DISCALCED CARMELITES

Br. Robert M. Sentman, OCD
514 Warren Street
Brookline, MA 02146
617-232-2237

Rev. John Melka, OCD
12455 Clayton Road
Box 3420
San Jose, CA 95116
408-251-1361

* *Members of NCRVD but no Community Description Page*

Vocation Director, OCD
Mt. St. Joseph
P.O. Box 3420
San Jose, CA 95156-3420

BROTHERS OF CHARITY

Br. Timothy Hartnett, FC
7720 Doe Lane
Philadelphia, PA 19118

MISSIONARIES OF CHARITY

Vocation Director
1600 Ingraham Street
Los Angeles, CA 90017

SERVANTS OF CHARITY

Rev. Germano Pegoraro, SC
1795 S. Sproul Road
Springfield, PA 19064
215-328-3406

CONGREGATION OF CHRISTIAN BROTHERS

Br. Vincent M. McNally, CFC
135 Glenwood Avenue
East Orange, NJ 07017
201-676-3334

Br. Kevin T. Barry, CFC
715 North Avenue
New Rochelle, NY 10801
914-636-2270

Br. Joseph M. Clark, CFC
21 Pryer Terrace
New Rochelle, NY 10804
914-636-6194

Br. Kenneth J. Kowalewski, CFC
440 N. Evergreen
Chandler, AZ 85224
602-963-3100

Br. F.C. Chapman, CFC
21 Pryer Terrace
New Rochelle, NY 10804

DE LASALLE CHRISTIAN BROTHERS

Vocation Director
P.O. Box A-D
St. Mary's College
Moraga, CA 94575
415-376-4461

Vocation Director
1000 McNeilly Road
Pittsburgh, PA 15226
412-561-2363

Vocation Director
200 De LaSalle Drive
Romeoville, IL 60441
312-242-1240

Vocation Director
635 Ocean Road
Narragansett, RI 02882
401-789-0244

Vocation Director
820 Newman Springs Road
Lincroft, NJ 07738
201-842-7420

Vocation Director
807 Summit Avenue
St. Paul, MN 55105
612-224-4318

Vocation Director, FSC
The St. Paul's School
917 South Jahncke Avenue
Covington, LA 70434
504-892-3200

Vocation Director, FSC
124 Moore Avenue
Toronto, ONT M4T 1V3
CANADA

Vocation Director, FSC
650 Parkway South
P.O. Box F-120
Memphis, TN 38104

BROTHERS OF CHRISTIAN INSTRUCTION

Br. Eugene Belisle, FIC
133 Granite Street
Worcester, MA 01604
617-756-6184

CISTERCIANS

Rev. Roch Kereszty, O.Cist
Our Lady of Dallas Abbey
Route 2, Box 1
Irving, TX 75062

CLARETIANS

Rev. Bruce Wellems, CMF
221 W. Madison Street
Room 850
Chicago, IL 60606
312-236-7782

Edward J. Colon
1119 Westchester Place
Los Angeles, CA 90019
213-SERVING

COLUMBAN FATHERS

*Rev. Denis Bartley, SSC
35-55 223rd Street
P.O. Box 607
New York, NY 11361
212-224-8080

*Rev. Robert J. Clark, SSC
Columban Fathers
St. Columban's, NE 68056
402-291-1920

COMBONI MISSIONARIES

Rev. Brian Quigley, MCCJ
Vocation Department
8108 Beechmont Avenue
Cincinnati, OH 45230
513-474-4997

CONSOLATA MISSIONARIES

*Rev. Van Hager, IMC
7110 Thomas Blvd.
Pittsburgh, PA 15208
412-241-3995

CROSIERS

Br. Emil Hartman, OSC
Crosier Seminary
Onamia, MN 56359
612-532-3103

Vocation Director
3204 E. 43rd Street
Minneapolis, MN 55406

DIOCESAN LABORER PRIESTS

Rev. Ovid Pecharroman
1372 Cranwood Drive
Columbus, OH 43229
614-436-5725

DIVINE WORD MISSIONARIES

Rev. Eric P. Vargas, SVD
807 N. Fresno Street
Los Angeles, CA 90063
213-261-3083

Rev. Patrick J. Wenrick, SVD
101 Park Street
Bordentown, NJ 08505
609-298-0549

Rev. George Bergin, SVD
P.O. Box M
Duxbury, MA 02331
617-585-2460

Rev. John Horstman, SVD
Rev. Dennis Rausch, SVD
Br. Andre Hotchkiss, SVD
Rev. Mark Schramm, SVD
Rev. Gilbert J. Gawlik, SVD
Divine Word College
Epworth, IA 52045
319-876-3332

Rev. Lloyd Cunningham, SVD
Divine Word Seminary
1338 Seminary Road
East Troy, WI 53120
414-642-3300

Rev. Elmer Elsbernd, SVD
Divine Word Seminary
Perrysburg, OH 43551

Rev. Walter Bracken, SVD
Divine Word Seminary
Bay St. Louis, MS 39520

DOMINICANS

Rev. Peter F. Witchousky, OP
1909 S. Ashland Ave.
Chicago, IL 60608
312-666-4500

Rev. Anthony R. Rosevear, OP
Box 3045
Oakland, CA 94609
415-658-8722

Rev. Greg Salomone, OP
Immaculate Conception Priory
487 Michigan Ave., NE
Washington, DC 20017

EDMUNDITES

Rev. Richard M. Myhalyk, SSE
Fairholt-So. Prospect Street
Burlington, VT 05401
802-864-7040

FRANCISCAN BROTHERS OF BROOKLYN

Br. Peter Dawson, OSF
St. Francis Monastery
133 Remsen Street
Brooklyn, NY 11201
718-858-8217

Br. Gerald Francis, OSF
St. Augustine School
63 Pequonnock Street
Bridgeport, CT 06604
203-367-5896

Br. Edward Sullivan, OSF
St. Mary of the Angels Friary
30 Ocean Avenue
St. Augustine, FL 32084
904-824-9695

BROTHERS OF THE POOR
OF ST. FRANCIS

*Br. Joel Stern, CFP
105 Valley Street
Burlington, IA 52601
319-752-2244

ORDER FRIARS MINOR-CAPUCHIN

Vocation Director
St. Francis High School
200 Foothill Blvd.
LaCanada, CA 91011
818-790-6319

Vocation Director
St. Francis Friary
Castlegate Avenue
Pittsburgh, PA 15226
412-531-4545

Vocation Director
St. Michael Friary
225 Jerome Street
Brooklyn, NY 11207
718-647-7371

Vocation Director
1820 Mt. Elliot Ave.
Detroit, MI 48207
313-579-2100

Vocation Director
4117 Walnut Street
Kansas City, MO 64111
816-531-2727

Vocation Director
St. Venantius Friary
P.O. Box 549
Orange, NJ 07051
201-672-8320

Vocation Director
5707 Bernal Drive
Dallas, TX 75212
214-688-1183

ORDER FRIARS MINOR-CONVENTUAL

Franciscan Vocation Office
St. Francis Friary
500 Todt Hill Road, Box M
Staten Island, NY 10304
718-981-3131

Franciscan Vocation Office
St. Joseph Cupertino Novitiate
12290 Folly Quarter Road
Ellicott City, MD 21043-1499
301-988-9822

Franciscan Vocation Office
Holy Cross Friary
P.O. Box 158
Mesilla Park, NM 88047
505-524-3688

Franciscan Vocation Office
Sacred Heart Friary
6107 N. Kenmore Ave., Box M
Chicago, IL 60660
312-764-8811

Franciscan Vocation Office
101 St. Anthony Drive
Box M
Mt. St. Francis, IN 47146
812-923-8145
812-923-8819

Franciscan Vocation Office
St. Hyacinth College & Seminary
Box M
Granby, MA 01033
413-467-7189

Franciscan Vocation Office
3210 62nd Avenue
Box M
Oakland, CA 94605
415-562-7693

Franciscan Vocation Office
St. Anthony-on-Hudson
Box M
Rensselaer, NY 12144
518-434-4625

ORDER OF FRIARS MINOR

Franciscan Vocation Office
Southwest Province
1705 Five Points Road, SW
Albuquerque, NM 87105
505-243-1369

Franciscan Vocation Office
St. Barbara Province
1500 34th Avenue
Oakland, CA 94601
415-536-1266

Franciscan Vocation Office
Holy Name Province
600 Soundview Avenue
Bronx, NY 10473
212-893-5550

Franciscan Vocation Office
Custody of the Holy Land
1400 Quincy Street, NE
Washington, DC 20017
202-526-6800

Franciscan Vocation Office
Holy Cross Commissariat
8500 West Cold Spring Road
Greenfield, WI 53228
414-321-1965

Franciscan Vocation Office
St. John the Baptist Province
10290 Mill Road
Cincinnati, OH 45231
513-825-1082

Franciscan Vocation Office
Assumption Province
2414 West Vliet Street
Milwaukee, WI 53205
414-933-1476

Franciscan Vocation Office
Sacred Heart Province
3320 Paschal Drive
Oak Brook, IL 60521
312-654-4075

Franciscan Vocation Office
Immaculate Conception Province
9 Herbert Street
Melrose, MA 02176
617-662-9310

Franciscan Vocation Office
Lithuanian Vicariate of St. Casimir
Kennebunkport, ME 04046
207-967-2011

Franciscan Vocation Office
Byzantine/Slavonic Rite
82 Ponus Ridge Road
New Canaan, CT 06840
203-966-5159

Franciscan Vocation Office
Custody of St. John Capistran
1290 Hornberger Avenue
Roebling, NJ 08554
609-499-1564

Franciscan Vocation Office
Custody of the Most Holy Savior
232 South Home Avenue
Pittsburgh, PA 15202
412-761-2550

Franciscan Vocation Office
Vicariate of Christ the King
Box 220
Lumsden, Sask., S9O 3C0
CANADA
306-731-2444

FRANCISCAN BROTHERS
OF THE HOLY CROSS

Br. Gerald Voycheck, FFSC
R.R. #1, Sangamon Ave., E
Springfield, IL 62707
217-544-4876

LITTLE BROTHERS OF ST. FRANCIS

Vocation Director, OSF
789 Parker Street
Mission Hill, MA 02120

THIRD ORDER REGULAR
OF ST. FRANCIS

Franciscan Vocation Office
Immaculate Conception Friary
2006 Edgewater Parkway
Silver Spring, MD 20903
301-445-0124

Directors of Vocations
St. Francis Monastery
Loretto, PA 15940
814-472-7000

Vocation Office
P.O. Box 890
Winchester, VA 22601
703-869-5250

GLENMARY HOME MISSIONERS

Vocation Director
P.O. Box 46404
Cincinnati, OH 45246
513-874-8900

MISSIONARIES OF HOLY APOSTLES

*Rev. Francis J. Fajella, MSsA
33 Prospect Hill Road
Cromwell, CT 06416
203-635-5311

HOLY CROSS BROTHERS

Br. David Baltrinic, CSC
Columba Hall
Notre Dame, IN 46556
219-239-7830

Br. Bernard Palmeri, CSC
Southwest Province of Brothers
127 S. San Augustine St.
San Antonio, TX 78237
512-435-2454

Br. John Zick, CSC
R.D. #3 Box 113
Valatie, NY 12184
518-784-3481
518-784-9632

HOLY CROSS FATHERS

Rev. James J. Doherty, CSC
835 Clinton Avenue
Box M
Bridgeport, CT 06604
203-367-7252

Rev. Charles E. Van Winkle, CSC
908 San Jacinto Street
Austin, TX 78701
512-476-5439

Rev. Andre Leveille, CSC
Box 451
Notre Dame, IN 46556
219-239-6385

MISSIONARIES OF THE HOLY FAMILY

Rev. Joseph P. Roelke, MSF
2500 Ashby Road
St. Louis, MO 63114
314-427-2172

Rev. Danny Hawkins, MSF
Holy Family House
470 Wilbrod Street
Ottawa, ONT K1N 6M8
613-233-4667

HOSPITALLER BROTHERS
OF ST. JOHN OF GOD

Br. Elias Edelen, OH
525 W. Acacia Street
Salinas, CA 93912
408-424-5277

Rev. Fintan Brennan Whitmore, OH
532 Delsea Drive
Westville Grove, NJ 08093
609-848-4141

JESUITS

Vocation Director
3301 SE 45th
Portland, OR 97206
503-774-5699

Vocation Director
7101 W. 80th Street
Los Angeles, CA 90045
213-642-3170
408-354-6143

Vocation Director
Jesuit Provincial Residence
500 S. Jefferson Davis Pkwy.
New Orleans, LA 70119-7192
504-821-0334

Vocation Director
2599 Harvard Road
Berkley, MI 48072
313-399-8132

Vocation Director
3700 W. Pine Blvd.
St. Louis, MO 63108
314-652-3700

Vocation Director
1035 Summit Avenue
St. Paul, MN 55105
612-224-5593

Vocation Director
509 N. Oak Park Avenue
Oak Park, IL 60302
312-626-7934

Vocation Director
393 Commonwealth Ave.
Boston, MA 02115
617-266-7233

Vocation Director
501 E. Fordham Road
Bronx, NY 10458
212-584-0300

Vocation Director
Loyola Center
St. Joseph's College
Philadelphia, PA 19131
215-879-7777

Vocation Director
69 Marmaduke Street
Toronto, ONT M6R 1T3
416-763-4664

Vocation Director
Noviciat des Jesuites
1308 Rue Sherbrooke
Montreal, QUE H2L 1M2
514-523-2955

CONGREGATION OF ST. JOSEPH

Rev. Leo A. Dechant, CSJ
4076 Case Road
Avon, OH 44011
216-934-6270

JOSEPHITE FATHERS AND BROTHERS

Rev. Laurence A. Schmitt, SSJ
1200 Varnum St., NE
Washington, DC 20017
202-526-3616

LASALETTE MISSIONARIES

LaSalette Vocation Directors
Seven Dolors Province
85 New Park Avenue
Hartford, CT 06106
203-232-3282

LaSalette Vocation Director
Immaculate Heart of Mary Province
P.O. Box 538
Attleboro, MA 02703
617-222-6682

LaSalette Vocation Director
Mary Queen of Peace Province
1607 East Howard Ave.
Milwaukee, WI 53207
414-769-7113

LaSalette Vocation Director
Mary Queen Province
3741 Laclede Avenue
St. Louis, MO 63108
314-652-9291

MARIANISTS

Pacific Province
Rev. John C. Rielly, SM
175 Phelan Avenue
San Francisco, CA 94112
415-586-8181

New York Province
Br. Frank J. O'Donnell, SM
4301 Roland Avenue
Baltimore, MD 21210
301-366-1300

Cincinnati Province
Br. Robert N. Wiethorn, SM
4435 E. Patterson Road
Dayton, OH 45430
513-253-4738

St. Louis Province
Rev. Adolf M. Windisch, SM
4538 Maryland Avenue
St. Louis, MO 63108
314-367-0390

MARIANNHILL MISSIONARIES

Rev. Thomas E. Szura, CMM
23715 Ann Arbor Trail
Dearborn Hgts., MI 48127
313-274-2893

MARIANS OF THE IMMACULATE
CONCEPTION

Rev. Joseph C. Dicine, MIC
Eden Hill
Stockbridge, MA 01262
413-298-3931

MARIST BROTHERS OF THE SCHOOLS

Marist Brothers
1900 Kingsley Road
Eugene, OR 97401
503-343-6332

Marist Brothers
1241 Kennedy Blvd.
Bayonne, NJ 07002
201-823-1115

Marist Brothers
4300 Murdock Avenue
Bronx, NY 10466
718-994-4227

Marist Brothers
300 Hampshire St.
Lawrence, MA 01841
617-682-0260

Marist Brothers
83-53 Manton Street
Jamaica, NY 11435
718-441-2100

Marist Brothers
3000 SW 87th Avenue
Miami, FL 33165
305-223-5650

Marist Brothers
4200 W. 115th Street
Chicago, IL 60655
312-881-6360

MARISTS-SOCIETY OF MARY

Marist Vocation Director
518 Pleasant Street
Framingham, MA 01701-2802

Marist Vocation Director
480 Northfield Road
Bedford, OH 44146

Marist Vocation Director
2335 Warring Street
Berkeley, CA 94704

MARYKNOLL MISSIONERS

Rev. John Harper, MM
Director of Admissions
Maryknoll, NY 10545
800-431-2008
914-941-7590

MISSIONHURST

*Rev. James P. Fischler, CICM
4651 N. 25th Street
Arlington, VA 22207
703-528-3800

MONTFORT MISSIONARIES

Montfort Missionaries
1302 Quincy Street, NE
Washington, DC 20017

Montfort Missionaries
P.O. Box 358
Port Jefferson, NY 11777

Montfort Missionaries
3636 North Market Street
St. Louis, MO 63113

NORBERTINES-DAYLESFORD ABBEY

Rev. Francis Dorff, O. Praem.
220 S. Valley Road
Paoli, PA 19301
215-648-0529

NORBERTINES-ST. NORBERT ABBEY

Rev. Gene E. Gries, O. Praem.
St. Norbert Abbey
1016 N. Broadway
DePere, WI 54115-2697
414-336-1321

MISSIONARY OBLATES OF MARY IMMACULATE

Rev. Peter Cortez, OMI
707 Jefferson Avenue
Oakland, CA 94607
415-444-8627

Rev. Manuel A. Mesa, OMI
666 S. Workman
San Fernando, CA 91340
415-452-1550

Rev. Richard M. Sudlik, OMI
391 Michigan Avenue, NE
Washington, DC 20017
202-529-5244

Rev. Dayne C. Ripellino, OMI
100 Cushing Street
Cambridge, MA 02138
617-547-4149

Rev. James A. Deegan, OMI
267 E. 8th Street
St. Paul, MN 55101
612-292-8622

Br. William L. Johnson, OMI
2104 Davenport
Omaha, NE 68102
402-346-5800

Rev. Roger Temme, OMI
St. Edward's University
3001 Congress, Box 722
Austin, TX 78704
512-443-4403
512-443-3732

Rev. Ramiro Cortez OMI
Rev. Charles Hammond, OMI
Rev. Ronald W. Walker, OMI
121 W. Woodlawn Ave.
San Antonio, TX 78212
512-736-4288

Rev. James A. Allen, OMI
5901 W. Main Street
Belleville, IL 62223
618-233-2991

OBLATES OF ST. FRANCIS DE SALES

Rev. Albert J. Smith, OSFS
2200 Kentmere Pkwy.
Box 1452
Wilmington, DE 19899
302-656-8529

Rev. John L. Graden, OSFS
2460 Parkwood Ave.
Toledo, OH 43620
419-243-5105

CONGREGATION OF THE ORATORY

Rev. Thomas A. Keiffer, CO
P.O. Box 1667
Monterey, CA 93940
408-313-0476

Br. Joseph Guyon, CO
P.O. Box 11586
Rock Hill, SC 29731
803-327-2097

BROTHERS OF OUR LADY, MOTHER OF MERCY

*Br. Anthony Peter Smulders, CFMM
7140 Ramsgate Avenue
Los Angeles, CA 90045
213-642-2823

PIME MISSIONARIES

*Rev. Timothy W. Sattler, PIME
2734 Seminary Road, SE
Newark, OH 43056
614-928-4246

PALLOTTINES

Vocation Director
P.O. Box 1838
P.G. Plaza
Hyattsville, MD 20782

Vocation Director
5424 W. Bluemound Road
Milwaukee, WI 53208

SERVANTS OF THE PARACLETE

Vocation Director
Foundation House
Jemez Springs, NM 87025

Vocation Director
Servants of the Paraclete
Brownshill
Stroud, GL6 8AS
ENGLAND

PASSIONISTS

Rev. Peter L. Berendt, CP
700 N. Sunnyside Avenue
Sierra Madre, CA 91024
213-681-9387

Rev. John R. Conley, CP
5700 N. Harlem Avenue
Chicago, IL 60631
312-631-6336

Br. Patrick G. Hanson, CP
5700 N. Harlem Ave.
Chicago, IL 60631
312-631-6336

SOCIETY OF ST. PAUL

Br. Kevin J. Cahill, SSP
Br. Peter Lyne, SSP
Pauline Priests and Brothers
2187 Victory Blvd.
Staten Island, NY 10314
718-761-0047

Rev. Joseph Triano, SSP
Pauline Priests and Brothers
7050 Pinehurst
Dearborn, MI 48126
313-582-2033

Br. Anthony Warren, SSP
Pauline Priests and Brothers
6746 Lake Shore Road
Derby, NY 14047
716-947-5407

PAULIST FATHERS

Rev. Thomas P. Hall, CSP
Director of Vocations
415 W. 59th Street
New York, NY 10019

PIARIST FATHERS

Rev. John G. Callan, Sch. P.
Devon Prep School
363 Valley Forge Road
Devon, PA 19333
215-687-0279

Rev. Charles W. Newburn, Sch. P.
Cardinal Gibbons High School
4601 Bayview Drive
Fort Lauderdale, FL 33308
305-771-6525

Rev. Richard S. Wyzykiewicz, Sch. P.
Calasanctius School
167 Windsor Avenue
Buffalo, NY 14209
716-885-8508

SOCIETY OF THE PRECIOUS BLOOD

Vocation Ministry Office
Province of the Pacific
2800 Milvia Street
Berkeley, CA 94703

Vocation Ministry Office
Kansas City Province
Ruth Ewing Road
Liberty, MO 64068

Vocation Ministry Office
Cincinnati Province
229 W. Anthony Street
Celina, OH 45822

REDEMPTORISTS

Rev. John Devin, CSSR
Mapleton Street
Suffield, CT 06078
203-668-7393

Rev. David L. Polek, CSSR
One Liguori Drive
Liguori, MO 63057
314-464-2501

Rev. Peter Schavitz, CSSR
Holy Redeemer College
Waterford, WI 53185
414-534-3191

Rev. Mark C. Scheffler, CSSR
6921 Chetwood
Houston, TX 77081
713-669-0144

Rev. Daniel Andree, CSSR
3577 High Point Road
Madison, WI 53711
608-833-1010

Rev. Joseph Krastel, CSSR
St. Alphonsus College
Suffield, CT 06078
203-668-7393

Vocation Director
St. Mary's Seminary
North East, PA 16428
814-725-9641

Vocation Director
Box 279
New Smyrna Bch, FL 32069
904-428-6426

Rev. James Garcia, CSSR
Box 34455
San Francisco, CA 94134
415-585-0188

RESURRECTIONISTS

Rev. James Antosz, CR
3633 N. California
Chicago, IL 60618
312-622-0477

Rev. Sam Restivo, CR
Resurrection College
Waterloo, ONT N2L 3G7
519-885-4950

Rev. Michael Mas, CR
3920 West Pine Blvd.
St. Louis, Mo 63108
314- 533-8880

Rev. Gregory Helminski, CR
2250 N. Latrobe Avenue
Chicago, IL 60639
312-622-0477

Rev. Eugene Majewski, CR
2710 S. Country Club Rd.
Woodstock, IL 60098
815-338-1032

BROTHERS OF THE SACRED HEART

New York Province
Br. Robert Ziobro, SC
Vocation Office
145 Plainfield Avenue
Metuchen, NJ 08840
201-548-2292

New England Province
Br. James A. Lambert, SC
Vocation Office
159 Earle Street
Woonsocket, RI 02895
401-766-9677

New Orleans Province
Br. Lee Barker, SC
Vocation Office
4601 Elysian Fields
New Orleans, LA 70122
504-282-2228

MISSIONARIES OF THE SACRED HEART

MSC Vocation Office
P.O. Box 97
Center Valley, PA 18034
215-282-1414

CONGREGATION OF THE SACRED HEARTS

Vocation Director
3 Adams Street, Box 111
Fairhaven, MA 02719
617-993-2442

Vocation Director
32481 Sage Road
Hemet, CA 92343
714-652-3126

MISSIONARIES OF THE SACRED HEARTS OF JESUS AND MARY

Rev. Robert T. McDade, MSSCC
2249 Shore Road
Linwood, NJ 08221
609-927-5600

SALESIANS

Rev. Joseph Boenzi, SDB
DeSales Hall
13856 Bellflower Blvd.
Bellflower, CA 90706
213-925-0963

Rev. Mark Hyde, SDB
Salesian Junior Seminary
334 Main Street
Goshen, NY 10924
914-294-5138

Rev. Richard McCormick, SDB
Salesians of Don Bosco
Filors Lane
W. Haverstraw, NY 10993
914-947-2200

Rev. Richard Wanner, SDB
Don Bosco Hall
1831 Arch Street
Berkeley, CA 94709
415-441-7144

Rev. Harold Danielson, SDB
St. Mary's Salesian School
5252 137th Avenue
Edmonton, ALB T5A 1C7
403-476-1946

Rev. Richard Authier, SDB
Residence Don Bosco
510 Rue Quebec
Sherbrooke, QUE J1H 3L8
819-562-0053

SALVATORIANS

Rev. Gregory Coulthard, SDS
1735 Hi Mount Blvd.
Milwaukee, WI 53208
414-258-1735

SCALABRINIANS

Vocation Coordinator
3800 W. Division
Stone Park, IL 60165
312-345-8270

Vocation Coordinator
168-41 84th Avenue
Jamaica, NY 11432
718-526-3917

Vocation Coordinator
35 Cedar Street
Framingham, MA 01701
617-875-8623

Vocation Coordinator
Calle del Parque 400
Apdo 5-272
Guadalajara, Jalisco 45040
MEXICO

Vocation Coordinator
226 St. George Street
Toronto, ONT M5R 2N5
CANADA
416-922-7349

SERVITES

Br. Dominic M. Monforti, OSM
Our Lady of Sorrows Monastery
3121 W. Jackson Blvd.
Chicago, IL 60612

Vocation Director
5210 Somerset Street
Buena Park, CA 90621-1498

SONS OF MARY, MISSIONARIES

Rev. John Coss, FMSI
567 Salem End Road
Framingham, MA 01701-5599
617-879-6711

SPIRITANS

Rev. Robert Spangenberg, CSSp
Rev. Thomas G. Schaefer, CSSp
Spiritan Vocation Office
Duquesne University
Pittsburgh, PA 15282
412-765-0733

Rev. Michael T. Grey, CSSp
P.O. Box BB
Indio, CA 92202
714-347-3507

SOCIETY OF ST. SULPICE

Director of Formation
5408 Roland Avenue
Baltimore, MD 21210
301-323-5079

THEATINE FATHERS

*Rev. Thomas D. McConnell, CR
Provincial House of St. Andrew
1050 S. Birch Street
Denver, CO 80222
303-692-8491
303-756-5522

TRAPPISTS

*Rev. Aquinas J. Keane, OCSO
St. Joseph's Abbey
Spencer, MA 01562
617-885-3901

Br. Hilary Carney, OCSO
New Melleray Abbey
Dubuque, IA 52001

TRINITY MISSIONS

Rev. Clif Marquis, ST
9001 New Hampshire Avenue
Silver Spring, MD 20903
301-434-6764

ORDER OF MOST HOLY TRINITY

Rev. William J. Moorman, OSST
P.O. Box 5719
Baltimore, MD 21208
301-484-2250

VIATORIANS

Rev. Joseph Lofy, CSV
651 W. Roscoe
Chicago, IL 60657
312-525-7733

VINCENTIANS

Rev. Anthony Kuzia, CM
Vincentian House
1109 Prospect Avenue
West Hartford, CT 06105
203-236-5255

Rev. Vincent J. O'Malley, CM
St. John's University
Grand Central & Utopia Pkwys.
Jamaica, NY 11439
718-990-6161

Vocation Director
1723 Pennsylvania Avenue
St. Louis, MO 63116
314-664-5905

Rev. Jeffrey L. Malpiede, CM
Vincentian Center
1302 Kipling Street
Houston, TX 77006
713-523-0767

Rev. Robert J. Jones, CM
649 W. Adams Blvd.
Los Angeles, CA 90007
213-749-1865

VOCATIONIST FATHERS

Rev. Edgar M. Da Cunha, SDV
442 Brinkerhoff Avenue
Palisades Park, NJ 07650
201-944-1154

XAVERIAN BROTHERS

*Br. John J. McDonald, CFX
704 Brush Hill Road
Milton, MA 02186-1399
617-333-0970

*Br. William Griffin, CFX
16 Wyndcrest Avenue
Catonsville, MD 21228
301-644-3300
301-788-4699

XAVERIAN MISSIONARIES

Vocation Director
12 Helene Court
Wayne, NJ 07470
201-942-2975

Vocation Director
101 Summer Street
Holliston, MA 01746
617-429-2144

Vocation Director
6838 S. 51st. Street
Franklin, WI 53132
414-421-0831

**Please Use
These Cards
for Additional
Information from
Dioceses
and/or
Religious
Communities
In Which
You Are
Interested**

- Fill in Non-Addressed Cards when requesting information from a specific Vocation Director. Address Card to person listed in this book

- To request information from several religious communities (please limit to 5 or less) mail card pre-addressed to National Conference of Religious Vocation Directors

For additional copies of MINISTRIES FOR THE LORD ($4.95 each, prepaid) order from your bookstore or direct from PAULIST PRESS, 997 Macarthur Boulevard, Mahwah, NJ 07430.

VOCATION PRAYER

Creator God,
  You have gifted me with life.
  Through Baptism, you call me each day
  to show your love in our world.
You want me to be happy.
Help me to choose a life work which
  will be in response to your love for me.
Give me the courage and the strength to
  serve you, my God, in whatever way
  you call me.

Sr. Roseann Kasayka, OSF

Please send . . .
. . . more information about the Church Vocation described on page _____ of MINISTRIES FOR THE LORD

Name _____ Age _____
Address _____
Telephone _____
City _____ State _____ Zip _____
Years of education completed _____
Name of Parish _____

(Please address other side of this card to vocation director listed in the Index of Directors. Attach stamp and mail)

Please send . . .
. . . more information about the Church Vocation described on page _____ of MINISTRIES FOR THE LORD

Name _____ Age _____
Address _____
Telephone _____
City _____ State _____ Zip _____
Years of education completed _____
Name of Parish _____

(Please address other side of this card to vocation director listed in the Index of Directors. Attach stamp and mail)

Please send . . .
. . . more information about the Church Vocation described on page _____ of MINISTRIES FOR THE LORD

Name _____ Age _____
Address _____
Telephone _____
City _____ State _____ Zip _____
Years of education completed _____
Name of Parish _____

(Please address other side of this card to vocation director listed in the Index of Directors. Attach stamp and mail)

Please Place Stamp Here

TO:

_____

_____

_____

Please Use These Cards for Additional Information from Dioceses and/or Religious Communities In Which You Are Interested

- Fill in Non-Addressed Cards when requesting information from a specific Vocation Director. Address Card to person listed in this book

Please Place Stamp Here

TO:

_____

_____

_____

- To request information from several religious communities (please limit to 5 or less) mail card pre-addressed to National Conference of Religious Vocation Directors

For additional copies of MINISTRIES FOR THE LORD ($4.95 each, prepaid) order from your bookstore or direct from PAULIST PRESS, 997 Macarthur Boulevard, Mahwah, NJ 07430.

Please Place Stamp Here

TO:

_____

_____

_____

VOCATION PRAYER

My Lord,
I want to listen to your call with all
my heart.
Then I can understand what it is you ask
_of me._
You need my hands to build,
My strength to support others,
My smile that others may laugh.
You need my entire being for the
good of the world.
In a personal way, you invite me to follow
you.
Be with me, and help me to choose how best
to serve you and your people.

Sr. Roseann Kasayka, OSF